THE NEW NURSING ASSISTANT STUDENT WORKBOOK AND SKILLS CHECKLISTS

Written by
Barbara Gillogly, Ph.D., Ed.

Revised and Updated by
Molly Conley, R.N., M.S.N. and John Shannon

MEDCOM TRAINEX®
6060 PHYLLIS DRIVE, CYPRESS, CA 90630
PHONE 800 877-1443 • FAX 714 898-4852
www.medcomRN.com

CNA533U
Revised and Printed 6/04, 4/05, 8/10
Companion to Textbook — 8th Edition

Production Management by Tina Armstrong.
Edited and revised by John Shannon.
Book design and layout by Patty Mago.
Project Management by Jon Haverstick.
Art by George Dimichina and Bob Story.
Photography by Ross Olson.

About the Author

Barbara Gillogly is the Director of the Gerontology Program at American River College in Sacramento, California.

Dr. Gillogly received her education at California State University, Sacramento, and the University of California, Davis with degrees in Psychology, Gerontology, and Human Development. Dr. Gillogly would like to thank Ann Jasper, R.N. for her invaluable advice and expertise.

Advice and technical expertise for the completion and updating of this manual have been provided by Molly Conley, RN, MSN. Ms. Conley is a California Director of Vocational Nursing and is responsible for renewal of the Certified Nursing Assistant and Home Health Aide programs. She teaches at the North Orange County Regional Occupational Program in Anaheim, California. She has completed post-graduate work in nursing at SUNY-Buffalo, and in nursing education at California State University, Long Beach, California State University, Fullerton, and California State Polytechnic University, Pomona.

Dedication

To the nursing assistant, the most important hands-on care giver in the long term care profession. Without your sincere dedication, devotion to your patients and desire to promote high quality care, it would be impossible for us to satisfy the social consciousness of the nation toward our frail and elderly patients.

TABLE OF CONTENTS

Chapter 1: The Role Of The Nursing Assistant 1

Chapter 2: What is Long-Term Care? 3

Chapter 3: The Rights of Residents 4

Chapter 4: Ethics And Confidentiality 5

Chapter 5: Abuse and Neglect 7

Chapter 6: Caring For Others And Dealing With Stress .9

Chapter 7: Documentation 10

Chapter 8: Admissions 12

Chapter 9: Disasters and Evacuations 13

Chapter 10: Transfers, Discharges, Homecare 15

Chapter 11: Anatomy and Physiology: The Skeletal And Muscular Systems 17

Chapter 12: Anatomy and Physiology: The Urinary System 19

Chapter 13: Anatomy and Physiology: The Integumentary System 21

Chapter 14: Anatomy and Physiology: The Cardiovascular System 23

Chapter 15: Anatomy and Physiology: The Respiratory System 25

Chapter 16: Anatomy and Physiology: The Endocrine System 27

Chapter 17: Anatomy and Physiology: The Sensory System 29

Chapter 18: Anatomy and Physiology: The Digestive System 31

Chapter 19: Anatomy and Physiology: The Nervous System 33

Chapter 20: Infection Control 35

Chapter 21: Optimum Levels Of Health 37

Chapter 22: Age-Specific Issues 38

Chapter 23: Communicating With The Residents 39

Chapter 24: Principles of Observation 41

Chapter 25: Measuring Weight And Height 42

Chapter 26: Measuring Vital Signs 44

Chapter 27: The "Fifth Vital Sign" — Pain 48

Chapter 28: Activities Of Daily Living 49

Chapter 29: Resident Activity Needs 51

Chapter 30: Physical Needs Of The Resident 52

Chapter 31: Resident Belongings And Prostheses 53

Chapter 32: The Environment of Care: Resident Safety .55

Chapter 33: Moving A Resident 58

Chapter 34: Ambulation 60

Chapter 35: Safety In Ambulation And Restraint 62

Chapter 36: Inactivity And Range Of Motion Exercises .64

Chapter 37: Pressure Ulcers And Positioning 65

Chapter 38:   Bed Making And Comfort Measures 68

Chapter 39:   Bathing The Resident 69

Chapter 40:   Personal Hygiene 71

Chapter 41:   Dressings And Bandages 73

Chapter 42:   IV Care And Tube Feeding 75

Chapter 43:   Basic Foods And Fluids 75

Chapter 44:   Feeding A Resident 78

Chapter 45:   Special Diets 80

Chapter 46:   Elimination Needs 81

Chapter 47:   Bladder And Bowel Care 84

Chapter 48:   Understanding Behavior 87

Chapter 49:   Remotivation 88

Chapter 50:   Psychosocial Needs 89

Chapter 51:   Socialization Needs 90

Chapter 52:   Intervention and Substance Abuse 91

Chapter 53:   Role Changes 92

Chapter 54:   Dementia And Confusion 93

Chapter 55:   Sexuality 95

Chapter 56:   Culture And Religion .96

Chapter 57:   Death And Dying 97

Chapter 58:   Using A Computer 99

Chapter 59:   Your Career in Healthcare 101

SKILLS CHECKLISTS 103

Admissions: Assisting with a Baseline Assessment (Chapter 8) 105

Admissions: Transfers, Discharges and Homecare (Chapter 10) 106

Infection Control (Chapter 20) 109

Measuring Weight and Height (Chapter 25) 111

Measuring Vital Signs (Chapter 26) 117

The Environment of Care: Resident Safety (Chapter 32) 126

Moving a Resident (Chapter 33) 127

Ambulation (Chapter 34) 133

Safety in Ambulation and Restraint (Chapter 35) 134

Inactivity and Range of Motion Exercises (Chapter 36) 138

Pressure Ulcers and Positioning (Chapter 37) 139

Bedmaking and Comfort Measures (Chapter 38) 142

Bathing the Resident (Chapter 39) 149

Personal Hygiene (Chapter 40) 157

Dressings and Bandages (Chapter 41) 164

IV Care and Tube Feeding (Chapter 42) 167

Feeding a Resident (Chapter 44) 169

Elimination Needs (Chapter 46) 173

Bladder and Bowel Care (Chapter 47) 178

Chapter 1: The Role of the Nursing Assistant

✎ Activity 1: Team Members

Check below the personnel who might be members of a healthcare team in a long-term care facility:

___ Registered Nurse.	___ Janitor.	___ Owner.
___ Dietician.	___ Family.	___ Clergy.
___ Nursing Assistant.	___ Driver.	___ Physical Therapist.
___ Cook.	___ Physician.	___ Carpenter.

✎ Activity 2: Role of Nursing Assistant

Check below the tasks that are important parts of your role as a nursing assistant:

___ Fulfilling responsibilities to employer.	___ Providing a safe environment.
___ Providing all medications and medical treatments.	___ Cooking meals.
___ Eye care.	___ Washing dishes.
___ Meeting the resident's physical needs.	___ Meeting the resident's psychosocial needs.

✎ Activity 3: Short Answers

Write short answers in the blanks below:

a. Bathing, oral hygiene and grooming are known as _____ _____ .

b. The need to feel secure or be treated with dignity or be recognized as an individual is a _____ .

c. Practicing fire safety and the use of side rails would be considered providing _____ .

d. Being dependable and relating well with others would be considered responsibilities to _____ .

✏ ACTIVITY 4: DAILY LIVING

Find and circle in the grid below six words or groups of words that refer to activities of daily living:

WORD LIST

BATHING
ORAL HYGIENE
GROOMING
DRESSING
TOILETING
FEEDING

```
F V G B G R E N C F G W D J G
E G G O L H R J M D P N F O F
E H T O I L E T I N G J S R K
D Q W E L H C W L J F G Q A D
I P V E R X G X E O F P C L R
N D J M O N P R P Q O D Q H M
G K F V I R K K O Z B R X Y N
J K B H J G S K U S L E W G T
T D T P A J S R V U L S F I Z
I A E T L S D L R U W S F E I
B V P I Y D A Y T Q G I I N Z
Q Y K X K E N K B O U N Q E E
K P W U D D P H Q D B G V Z I
X N M G R O O M I N G E J L C
V P T K F V S U N A P Q W H G
```

✏ ACTIVITY 5: CROSSWORD

Fill in the crossword below with the words that fit the definitions:

ACROSS

1. Abbreviation for certified nursing assistant.

4. Official statement of what will or will not be done.

6. Describing a person's mental or emotional processes.

DOWN

2. The act of walking.

3. Ability to experience the feelings of others.

5. Sorrow for the suffering of others.

You may use some of the following words:

Ambulation	CNA	Depression	Policy
Autocracy	DNA	Empathy	Psychosocial
Compassion	Departure	Leverage	RN

Chapter 2: What is Long-Term Care?

ACTIVITY 1: FORMS OF CARE

Draw a line from each form of care in the left column to the most likely caregiver(s) in the right column:

a. Recreation   Dietician.

b. Medical Care   The CNA.

c. Personal Care   Physical and Occupational Therapists.

d. Nutrition   Activity Coordinator and family.

e. Therapy   Nurse and CNA.

f. The largest amount of direct care for one resident   Physician and Charge Nurse.

ACTIVITY 2: TYPES OF FACILITIES

Rank the following types of facilities in the order of the amount of medical care available. Put a 1 beside the facility that offers the <u>most complete</u> medical care, then 2, etc:

___ Subacute Care Unit.   ___ Board and Care Facility.

___ Adult Day Care.   ___ Hospital.

___ Long-term Care Facility.   ___ Assisted Living Facility.

ACTIVITY 3: SHORT ANSWERS

Write short answers in the blanks below:

a. A facility that provides 24-hour care for the terminally ill is called a _____.

b. Nursing care provided in the home is often called _____.

c. Long-term care facilities are often called _____.

d. A person who is treated without being admitted to a facility is called _____.

e. A federal law that regulates long-term care is often referred to as _____.

ACTIVITY 4: MANAGED CARE

Draw a line from the description of a form of managed care in the left column to the term for that care in the right column:

a. An institution that agrees to provide all a person's health care for an agreed amount.   DRGs

b. A plan that pays medical costs as long as the person goes to a provider on a set list.   HMO

c. A plan that covers a specific disease.   Disease Management

d. A set amount that the government will pay for a specific condition.   PPO

Chapter 3: The Rights of Residents

ACTIVITY 1: RESIDENT RIGHTS

Check below the rights that a resident is guaranteed:

___ The right to refuse treatment.

___ The right to free treatment.

___ The right to abuse other residents.

___ The right to privacy.

___ The right to personal possessions.

___ The right to make loud noises at any hour.

___ The right to have access to a telephone.

___ The right to participate in social activities that interfere with others.

___ The right to refuse to perform work for the facility.

___ The right to organize resident groups.

ACTIVITY 2: LEGAL TERMS

Draw a line from each legal term in the left column to the appropriate definition in the right column:

a. Assault   Obtaining permission to perform a procedure after explaining risks.

b. Battery   The actual use of violence.

c. Elder abuse   A guardian who looks out for the rights of others.

d. Informed consent   Mistreatment of older people.

e. Malpractice   The threat or use of violence.

f. Ombudsman   Neglect or wrong treatment by a professional.

✏ ACTIVITY 3: ADVANCE DIRECTIVES

Check all the statements below that are TRUE of an advance directive:

___ It will be the same for all residents in a facility.

___ It defines steps to be taken or avoided as the person approaches death.

___ It is also called a legal will.

___ It will be stored in the administrator's office.

___ It is also called a living will.

___ It will be stored with the resident's chart.

___ It will always call for CPR in the event of heart stoppage.

___ It can be changed orally at any time by the resident.

___ It is a legal requirement in most cases and must be followed.

✏ ACTIVITY 4: DISCRIMINATION

Find and circle in the grid below six words or phrases that refer to forms of discrimination that are illegal:

WORD LIST

AGE

SEX

RACE

RELIGION

ETHNIC ORIGIN

PHYSICAL HANDICAP

```
D W R Z H Q B P P K W N L J A U B
R Y A X J X X W H H R A C E F I F
E R I N E T E Y Y K G B W M M I U
L H J S K K P N S Z P K P A C E X
I W H Y Z Z Z S I P B C F O L T Q
G N G P M R O D C Q A X M H W H Q
I G R E A N Z N A B C Z O M N N U
O R V B I N E Q L Q L S Y X X I C
N S I A L L Q Q H J T B E A W C Q
S P A F G I F G A W X L Z N M O P
F E O A L E D G N Z L A Q T W R Z
U W E X D A T U D P K S G D O I G
A Y D B X J P E I O L I R X V G U
H A Z F Y X V E C D F L S H E I N
Q G F Z K K J F A F A F K Z Y N W
J U Z G W G C R P D D H B R L E U
A B A F P V N C U C K Z L A K U M
```


Chapter 4: Ethics and Confidentiality

✏ ACTIVITY 1: ETHICS

Check the people below who are protected by your ethical behavior at work:

___ Residents you work with.

___ Your state senate.

___ Yourself.

___ Local police.

___ Neighbors.

___ Your facility.

ACTIVITY 2: ETHICAL BEHAVIOR AT WORK

Check the acts below that would be considered ethical:

___ Having a positive attitude at work.

___ Remaining neat and tidy.

___ Taking care of your own personal needs first.

___ Playing a practical joke on one of the residents.

___ Being courteous even if a resident is rude to you.

___ Ignoring the needs of a resident who is not assigned to you.

___ Taking a quick nap on duty when you are very tired.

___ Respecting the residents as individuals.

___ Asking the charge nurse for assistance when you don't know what to do.

___ Keeping information about a resident confidential.

ACTIVITY 3: ETHICAL BEHAVIOR TO YOUR EMPLOYER

Check below the acts toward your employer that are NOT considered ethical:

___ Leaving work a little early to go shopping.

___ Arriving on time and ready to work.

___ Ignoring the needs of other staff members.

___ Following the instructions of your supervisor.

___ Being absent only in illness or emergency.

___ Calling in absent just as your shift starts.

___ Following a supervisor's instructions without question, even if it may harm a resident.

___ Being helpful to other staff members.

ACTIVITY 4: ETHICS CROSSWORD

Fill in the crossword below with the words that fit the definitions:

ACROSS

2. Federal law related to confidentiality.

4. Failure to give proper care, resulting in harm.

DOWN

1. Something false and damaging that is spoken.

3. A group of moral principles.

5. Moral principles or values.

6. Something false and damaging in writing.

You may use some of the following words:

Battery	Ethics	Libel	Trust
Code	Immoral	Negligence	Unhappiness
Decode	Legal	Slander	HIPAA

Chapter 5: Abuse and Neglect

✎ ACTIVITY 1: FORMS OF ABUSE AND NEGLECT

Write the letter A beside each activity below that could be considered abuse. Write N beside each activity that could be considered Neglect.

___ A slap in the face.

___ Stealing property.

___ Leaving a bedridden person alone for hours.

___ Calling someone an offensive name.

___ Withholding food.

___ Using restraints for convenience.

___ Never combing the hair of a person who can't comb her own hair.

✎ ACTIVITY 2: SIGNS OF ABUSE

Check below the signs that might likely indicate abuse.

___ A puncture wound.

___ A bright smile.

___ Bruises.

___ Interest in community activities.

___ Strap marks.

___ Hides from visitors.

___ Friendliness with other residents.

___ Is afraid to be alone.

✎ ACTIVITY 3: SIGNS OF NEGLECT

Check below the signs that might likely indicate neglect.

___ Body lice.

___ Gaining weight.

___ Becoming a leader with other residents.

___ Poor appetite activities.

___ Pressure sores.

___ Obsessively opening drawers.

___ Friendliness with other residents.

___ Unclean body.

Find and circle in the grid below seven words or phrases that refer to basic or emotional needs:

WORD LIST

DEHYDRATION
THREATS
BURNS
WEIGHT LOSS
PRESSURE
SORES
HIDING
BRUISES

```
R N P F A Q D D W X N Q X U L V Q J A
W E I G H T L O S S J A Q T X G G D E
Z I K Q L W S K Z J Y S Z H D N H D T
R D U C F B M S E S I U R B B I Y Y A
F D E R Q Y D P X R V G L P C D A C G
R W A H G M B U C G O M N R Z I Y C V
Z H V Y Y D B E J Z O G A E U H P T H
H Q X O N D U G Y G F C W S G K R N V
B N N X M G R U N M J C F S J Q E J H
S K G A P T N A M B Z T T Y Z H S P J
P V D Q R J S O T E I A K Y R Z S L E
M Y R Y J O Z F V I E S G K N N U T P
U P K T M B J W F R O V O K B V R F Y
B A O I N Z H P H D A N P A Q J E L L
I V Y S D D W T J F S X X D W Q S K Z
A Y G G X G D M Q U W F G Z O B O P V
S F C P I H U S I O A W G M Q K R V L
C B W R V C O Q M E V O M Q H E E R S
I V G Q L K J I A O C C Y C G B S E O
```

Chapter 6: Caring for Others and Dealing with Stress

ACTIVITY 1: BASIC NEEDS

Find and circle in the grid below seven words or phrases that refer to basic or emotional needs:

WORD LIST

AIR

WATER

FOOD

SHELTER

FEELING LOVED

FEELING

 WORTHWHILE

FEELING SAFE

```
Z I U T S G F F L I F J E F H S A J H
V S R P U G N X M P B L Q U H K F S Z
B H H J F E E L I N G S A F E C E E C
I E V V N G S J O Q S I M T D C E W G
R L T U L H N R H V X D R Y P X L C J
L T Z P T G I H D Y M M N G Q V I O T
N E R J Y A P M W Z S Y A J W I N A N
F R T L U A W F U L Q Y G K G W G Y O
G A Y A T Z T F O M Z D Y O I S L W G
Q M O W M R X P A O M S Z N S N O N Z
S B Z R E Q W N N Y D J I J I G V C V
O J M T P X V T Z N K K Z R E M E F B
S Z A S V G A V V W H G E D X I D R U
T W T I L Z O Z F C E K R Y U G T A C
S N W C I T G Q S T M U J E I F E Z S
G J N Q V S W U B J F M U X I L O V L
F A S F Z L Q Y Y V I O E V R L U Y L
F E E L I N G W O R T H W H I L E Y D
U E Y X J X C V P M K V T C U K B E J
```

ACTIVITY 2: CAUSES OF STRESS

Check below the things that are likely to increase the stress in your life:

___ Feeling unliked or misunder-stood.

___ Getting plenty of sleep.

___ Dieting.

___ A personal crisis.

___ Eating well.

___ Having a comfortable income.

___ Lack of exercise.

___ Caring for a big family and working.

___ A loving home life.

___ Loss of income.

___ Moving.

ACTIVITY 3: HUMAN DIFFERENCES

Write the letter D by each trait below in which people can be different. Write an S by each trait in which people are more likely to be the same:

___ Need to eat daily.

___ Religious beliefs.

___ Handicaps.

___ Need for air.

___ Age.

___ Need for respect.

___ Stage of life.

___ Customs.

___ Need to feel safe.

___ Favorite foods.

✏ ACTIVITY 4: DEALING WITH STRESS

Check below any activities that are likely to help you deal effectively with stress:

___ Listening to relaxing music.

___ Being upset at your family.

___ Meditation.

___ Sitting calmly for a few minutes with your feet up.

___ Bottling up your problems.

___ Listening to loud fast music.

___ Talking over your problems with a friend.

___ Getting regular exercise.

Chapter 7: Documentation

✏ ACTIVITY 1: TERMINOLOGY

Draw a line from each term in the left column to the definition in the right column that best fits that term:

a. Nursing care plan

b. Objective observation

c. Chart

d. Kardex

e. Subjective observation

f. Documentation

An observation based on what you think.

Written information in the medical record.

The complete plan of care for a resident.

An observation based on what you can see.

A conveniently located file that summarizes the care plan.

All the health information on one person.

✏ ACTIVITY 2: NURSING CARE PLAN

Draw a line from the item in the left column to an appropriate entry in the right column for that item:

a. Problem

b. Short-term goal

c. Long-Term goal

d. Nursing approach

Ambulation three times daily. Monitor progress.

Can walk unaided.

Walk length of hall with assistance.

Unable to walk unaided.

✏ ACTIVITY 3: RULES FOR CHARTING

Check below the rules for charting that are CORRECT:

___ Entries must be written in erasable pencil.

___ Every sheet of the chart must have the resident's name and identifying information.

___ Use ditto marks only if the information is exactly the same as above.

___ Use approved medical abbreviations.

___ Entries should be brief and complete.

___ Leave one blank line between entries.

___ If you make a mistake use "white-out" to cover it over.

___ Every entry must be signed.

___ Entries must be in chronological order.

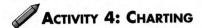

Circle any inappropriate or mistaken entries on the chart page below. Draw a line from each mistake to the white space below and write what is wrong with that entry:

Very Busy Nursing Home			Resident: B10345	
			Physician: M. Black M.D.	
Name: Brown, Jane			Room 21B	

Date	Time	Obs.	Treat	Remarks / Signature
1-1-02	7:00	BP too high	Notify charge nurse	Anne Taylor, CNA
1-1-02	7:15	Hated breakfast		Anne Taylor, CNA
1-1-02	8:00	Complained of pnfl stool		Anne Taylor, CNA
1-1-02	9:15	C/o "pain"	Notify charge nurse	Anne Taylor, CNA
1-1-02	10:30		Ambulated two lengths of hall.	Anne Taylor, CNA
1-1-02	11:30	~~Try to~~ Took nap		Anne Taylor, CNA

Write below anything that is wrong at the points indicated:

a._____

b._____

c._____

d._____

e._____

f._____

g._____

ACTIVITY 5: OBJECTIVE AND SUBJECTIVE

Below are several observations. Write an O by each one that appears to be objective and S by each one that appears to be subjective:

___ Resident was too hot.

___ Resident had torn shirt pocket.

___ Resident had temperature of 98.9 degree F.

___ Resident complained of nausea.

___ Resident purposely dropped food tray when no one was in the room.

___ Resident was not at therapy today.

___ Resident wasn't trying to ambulate.

___ Resident was irritable.

___ Resident had blood pressure of 130/80.

Chapter 8: Admissions

ACTIVITY 1: WELCOMING A NEW RESIDENT TO THE FACILITY

Check below appropriate actions to help welcome a new resident to the facility:

___ Joke and tease the resident.

___ Introduce yourself.

___ Learn the resident's name.

___ Leave the resident alone in the lobby to get used to the facility.

___ Introduce the resident to other residents.

___ Make up a pet name for the resident.

___ Greet family and friends.

ACTIVITY 2: WELCOMING A NEW RESIDENT TO THE ROOM

Check below appropriate actions to help welcome a new resident to the room:

___ Tell the resident where it is and leave the him or her alone to find it.

___ Show the resident how to make the bed.

___ Help the resident make a list of personal possessions.

___ Introduce the resident to roommates or neighbors.

___ Turn out the lights and have the resident find his or her way around in the dark.

___ Explain facility rules and mealtimes.

___ Take away any personal items.

___ Explain controls for the TV and light switches.

ACTIVITY 3: PREPARING THE ROOM

Check below items that a room kit would likely include:

___ A basin.

___ A towel.

___ A hammer and tool kit.

___ Water pitcher and glass.

___ A CD player.

___ A small refrigerator.

___ Soap and washcloth.

___ A stapler.

✏ ACTIVITY 4: ADMISSION CROSSWORD

Fill in the crossword below with the items useful for making the following assessments in a baseline assessment:

ACROSS

1. Heart sounds

4. Counting pulse

5. Temperature

DOWN

1. Measuring weight

2. Testing urine

3. Blood pressure

You may use some of the following words:

Blood pressure gauge	Scale	Syringe	Toothbrush
Comb	Specimen cup	Tape measure	Tongue depressor
Metronome	Stethoscope	Thermometer	Watch

Chapter 9: Disasters and Evacuation

✏ ACTIVITY 1: DISASTER DEFINITIONS

Draw a line from each expression in the left column to the definition in the right column that best fits that term:

a. Disaster — An event in which you can expect to see many emergency patients from outside the facility.

b. Natural disaster — Any event that disrupts the normal activities of your institution or community.

c. Mass-casualty disaster — A list of supplies and what to do in an emergency situation.

d. Disaster plan — An event such as a fire, flood or earthquake.

✏️ ACTIVITY 2: COMMUNITY AND INSTITUTIONAL DISASTERS

Write the letter C beside events below which are likely to be community disasters. Write the letter I beside events that may be internal institutional disasters.

___ A tornado.

___ A poisoning.

___ The crash of a large airliner.

___ A hurricane.

___ A terrorist incident.

___ Computer failure.

___ A room fire.

___ A large epidemic

✏️ ACTIVITY 3: DISASTER PLAN

Check below the four main parts of a disaster plan.

___ Obedience.

___ Easing the disaster.

___ Preparation.

___ Speed.

___ Fire extinguishers.

___ Recovery.

___ Computers.

___ Response.

✏️ ACTIVITY 4: TRANSFER OR EVACUATION

In the event it becomes necessary to transfer patients within the institution in a disaster such as an earthquake, check the appropriate actions below.

___ Issue extra blankets to keep people warm.

___ Open all doors and windows.

___ Close drapes.

___ Close all fire doors.

___ Turn out electric lights and use candles.

___ Keep people separate.

___ Reassure everyone that all is well.

ACTIVITY 5: DISASTER CROSSWORD

Fill in the crossword below with the words that match these definitions:

ACROSS

1. To remove all residents from a facility to avoid danger.
3. A victim of a disaster.
4. A disaster involving large amounts of water.
6. A disaster involving high rotating wind.

DOWN

2. The signal given that it is safe to return to an area.
5. An explosive device often used by terrorists.

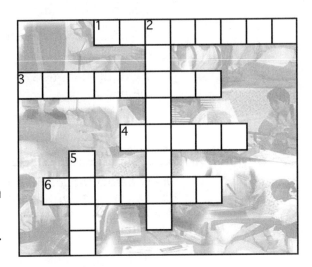

You may use some of the following words:

Airplane	Criminal	Flood	Response
All clear	Disaster	Hurricane	Tornado
Bomb	Epidemic	Preparation	Train wreck
Casualty	Evacuate	Resident	

Chapter 10: Transfers, Discharges, and Homecare

ACTIVITY 1: REASONS FOR TRANSFER

Check below likely reasons for initiating a room transfer:

___ The physician ordered it.

___ The resident may need oxygen and the room has no oxygen outlet.

___ You have decided to move the resident for your convenience.

___ The resident has requested it.

___ The resident has run out of money and is being moved to a cheaper room.

___ The resident may be discharged.

___ The resident is hard to get along with.

ACTIVITY 2: BEFORE A TRANSFER

Check below any activities you would likely perform before a transfer:

___ Repaint the room.

___ Get permission from the resident or family.

___ Speak to the nurse or CNA in the new area.

___ Hold a transfer party.

___ Tell all the neighbors.

___ Bring the CNA from the new area to meet the resident.

___ Sell off any unnecessary belongings.

___ Explain to the resident what is happening.

ACTIVITY 3: ASSISTING WITH TRANSFER

Below are some of the steps involved in a room transfer. Put them in the order you would perform them. Write the number 1 by the first step, etc:

___ Check the resident's ID.

___ Collect medications and the chart.

___ Explain what you are doing.

___ Obtain wheelchair, bed or cart.

___ Perform the transfer.

___ Prepare the new room.

ACTIVITY 4: REASONS FOR DISCHARGE

Write below three reasons you can think of for a resident to be discharged:

_____

_____

_____

ACTIVITY 5: TERMS

Draw a line from each term in the left column to the best definition for that term in the right column:

a. Client

b. Discharge

c. Home care

d. Home Health Assistant

e. Transfer

Care provided in a person's own home.

Steps to move someone to a new room.

Steps to release someone from a facility.

A person receiving care in his or her own home.

A nursing assistant who provides care in a person's home.

Chapter 11: Anatomy and Physiology: The Skeletal and Muscular Systems

ACTIVITY 1: THE SKELETON

Some of the bones of the skeleton are indicated below. Write the names of these bones on the lines provided:

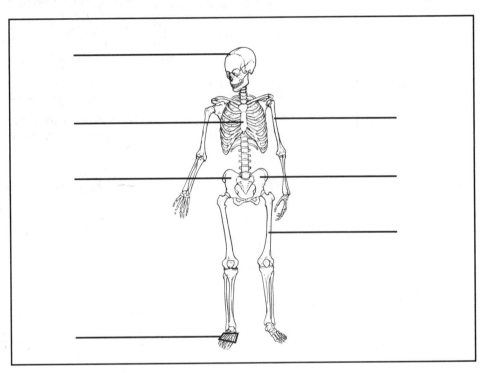

ACTIVITY 2: SKELETAL ABNORMALITIES

Draw a line from each term in the left column to the best definition for that term in the right column:

a. Bursitis   Inflammation of the joints.

b. Dislocation   Torn or stretched ligaments or tendons.

c. Osteoarthritis   An inflammation of the cartilage pad at a joint.

d. Osteoporosis   Deterioration of the cartilage at a joint.

e. Rheumatoid
 arthritis   Change in the normal alignment of bones at a joint.

f. Sprain   The bones lose calcium and become brittle.

✏ Activity 3: Muscles

Some of the more common muscles are indicated below. Write the names of these muscles on the lines provided:

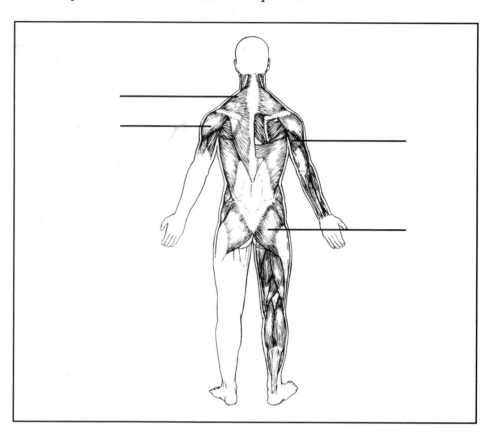

✏ Activity 4: Muscle types

Draw a line from each muscle type in the left column to its function in the right column:

a. Cardiac muscle   Moves internal organs.

b. Smooth muscle   Moves parts of the body.

c. Striated muscle   Contracts the heart.

ACTIVITY 5: MUSCLE ABNORMALITIES CROSSWORD

Fill in the crossword below with the muscular abnormalities that match these definitions:

ACROSS

1. A disease of the nerves that control muscles.

4. Wasting away of muscle tissue.

DOWN

1. Progressively crippling disease that causes weakness.

2. Loss of voluntary control over a muscle.

3. Permanent shortening of a muscle.

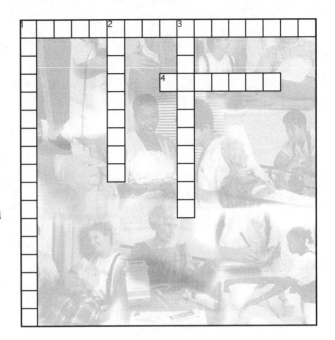

You may use some of the words below:

Atrophy	Contracture	Multiple sclerosis	Paralysis
Anomie	Deltoid	Muscular dystrophy	Polio
Anxiety	Dislocation	Osteoporosis	Sepsis

Chapter 12: Anatomy and Physiology: The Urinary System

 **ACTIVITY 1: THE URINARY SYSTEM**

Parts of the urinary system are indicated below. Write the names of these parts on the lines provided:

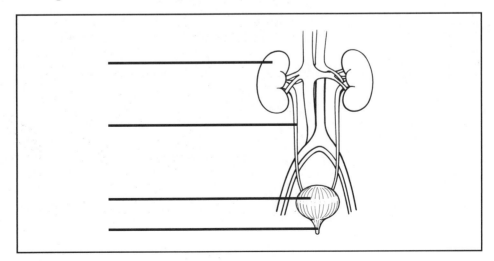

✏ ACTIVITY 2: KIDNEYS

Check the statements below that are TRUE of the kidneys:

___ The body contains three kidneys.

___ A kidney weighs about 12 ounces.

___ The kidneys are on either side of the spine.

___ We can live with only one kidney.

___ Each kidney contains about a thousand nephrons.

___ The kidneys filter wastes out of the blood.

___ The kidneys excrete urine.

___ The kidneys manufacture blood.

✏ ACTIVITY 3: THE BLADDER

Check the statements that are TRUE of the bladder:

___ The bladder collects urine before excreting it from the body.

___ The bladder filters wastes out of the blood.

___ The bladder is a fixed size.

___ Bladder walls contain receptors that signal when it is full.

___ Normal urine contains a little blood.

___ A full bladder is usually signaled at about 250 to 300 cc.

___ The bladder contains nephrons.

✏ ACTIVITY 4: SHORT ANSWERS

Fill in the blanks with the correct word or phrase:

a. The tube that carries urine out of the body is called the _____.

b. An infection in the kidney is called _____.

c. An infection in the bladder is called _____.

d. It is important to drink about _____ glasses of water a day.

e. To prevent infection, wipe urinary and anal areas _____.

ACTIVITY 5: INCONTINENCE

Check below any problems that may cause incontinence:

___ Tumors or trauma.

___ Urethra losing the ability to expand or contract.

___ Heart disease.

___ Medications.

___ Drinking too little water.

___ Confusion or disorientation.

___ Tuberculosis.

___ Progressive chronic diseases.

ACTIVITY 6: THE MALE URINARY SYSTEM

Parts of the male urinary system are indicated below. Write the names of these parts on the lines provided:

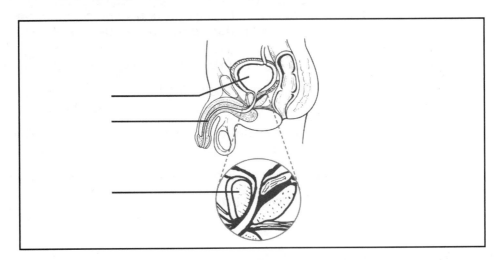

Chapter 13: Anatomy and Physiology: The Integumentary System

ACTIVITY 1: THE INTEGUMENTARY SYSTEM

Parts of the skin are indicated below in cross section. Write the names of these parts on the lines provided:

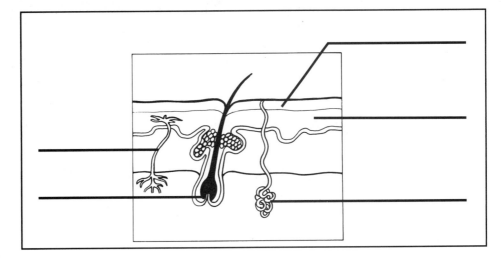

ACTIVITY 2: FUNCTIONS OF THE INTEGUMENTARY SYSTEM

Check below the functions of the integumentary system:

___ Helps the muscles move.

___ Detects pain.

___ Carries urine.

___ Regulates body temperature.

___ Protects body from dirt and germs.

___ Removes carbon dioxide from the body.

___ Prevents osteoporosis.

___ Produces Vitamin D.

___ Eliminates some wastes from body.

___ Produces Vitamin C.

ACTIVITY 3: DERMIS AND EPIDERMIS

By every statement below that is true of the Epidermis, write the letter E. By every statement that is true of the Dermis, write the letter D:

___ The inner layer of the skin.

___ The layer where blood vessels are found.

___ Cells are constantly dying and being shed.

___ Make up the soles of the feet.

___ The thicker layer of the skin.

___ The outer layer of the skin.

___ The layer visible from outside the body.

___ The layer where sweat glands are found.

___ The layer where nerves are found.

ACTIVITY 4: SHORT ANSWERS

Fill in the blanks with the correct word or phrase:

a. _____ helps regulate body temperature.

b. Oil glands _____ the skin.

c. Hair grows from _____.

d. _____ and _____ are appendages to the skin.

ACTIVITY 5: SKIN ABNORMALITIES CROSSWORD

Fill in the crossword below with the skin abnormalities that match these definitions:

ACROSS

2. Reddish patches with scales, often on knees or elbows.

4. Blue or gray skin due to lack of oxygen.

5. Redness of the skin.

DOWN

1. Scaly painful patches, often on sides.

2. Areas of skin that redden and then break open due to constant pressing.

3. Dry, red scaly patches.

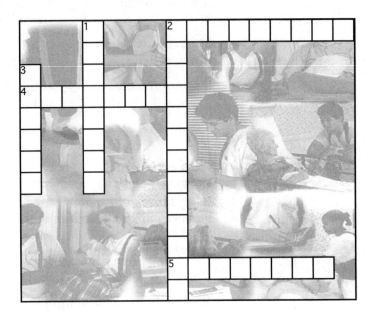

You may use some of the following words:

Atrophy	Eczema	Paralysis	Protein
Anemia	Erythema	Pressure sores	Shingles
Cyanosis	Osteoporosis	Psoriasis	Sepsis

Chapter 14: Anatomy and Physiology: The Cardiovascular System

 ## ACTIVITY 1: LOCATION OF THE HEART

This is the ribcage. Draw a shape on this diagram that shows the approximate size and position of the heart:

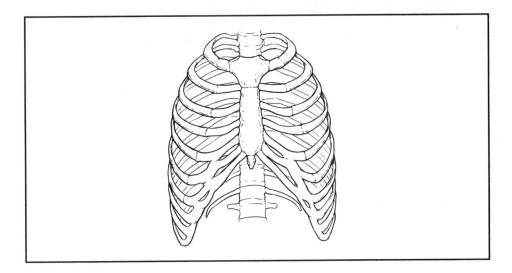

ACTIVITY 2: THE CARDIOVASCULAR SYSTEM

Check below the statements that are TRUE of the cardiovascular system:

___ It includes the heart.

___ It signals when the bladder is full.

___ It carries urine.

___ It carries oxygen to the cells.

___ It includes the lymph vessels.

___ It carries waste products away from the cells.

___ It filters the blood.

___ It lubricates the skin.

___ It includes the blood vessels.

___ It includes the blood.

ACTIVITY 3: ARTERIES AND VEINS

By every statement below that is true of the Arteries, write the letter A. By every statement that is true of the Veins, write the letter V:

___ Carry oxygen-rich blood.

___ Carry blood that is bright red.

___ Carry blood that is dark red.

___ Carry blood out to all parts of the body.

___ Receive blood from veinules.

___ Carry blood to arterioles.

___ Are elastic and can constrict or relax.

___ Carry blood from the body to the heart.

___ Carry oxygen-poor blood.

ACTIVITY 4: BLOOD

Check below the components of the blood:

___ Platelets.

___ Oxygen.

___ Capillaries.

___ Ureters.

___ Red blood cells.

___ White blood cells.

___ Urine.

___ Blue blood cells.

___ Plasma.

___ Lymph.

ACTIVITY 5: CARDIOVASCULAR DISEASES

Draw a line from each cardiovascular disease in the left column to the definition of that disease in the right column:

a. Angina

Sudden stop of blood supply to an area of the brain.

b. Arrythmias

Death of tissue in the heart.

c. Arteriosclerosis

Acute pain in the chest.

d. Congestive heart failure

Hardening of the arteries.

e. Stroke

Abnormal patterns of the heartbeat.

f. Heart attack

Gradual loss of the heart's ability to pump blood.

ACTIVITY 6: AGE-RELATED CHANGES

Below is one age-related change to the cardiovascular system. Write three more in the spaces provided:

The blood vessels thicken.

_____

_____

_____

Chapter 15: Anatomy and Physiology: The Respiratory System

ACTIVITY 1: THE RESPIRATORY SYSTEM

Parts of the respiratory system are indicated below. Write the names of these parts on the lines provided:

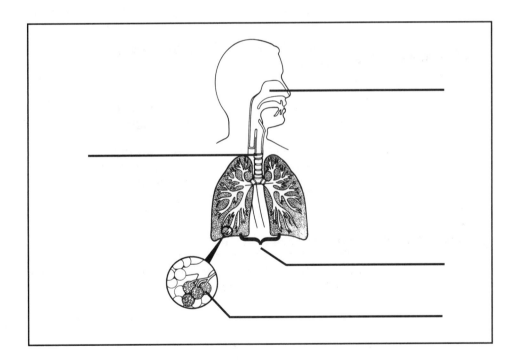

ACTIVITY 2: SHORT ANSWERS

Fill in the blanks with the appropriate word or phrase:

a. Breathing in is called _____; breathing out is

   called _____.

b. The main function of the respiratory system is to exchange the gas

   _____ for _____.

c. If small particles of food enter the airway, it is called

   _____.

d. Foreign matter is swept out of the lungs by _____.

e. The large muscular organ that helps the chest expand and contract

   is the _____.

ACTIVITY 3: AGE-RELATED CHANGES

Check below age-related changes to the respiratory system:

___ Lungs lose their elasticity.

___ Increased resistance to disease.

___ Mucous becomes thicker.

___ Air flows faster.

___ The body no longer needs oxygen.

___ Ribcage becomes more rigid.

___ More carbon dioxide is carried by the lungs.

___ Stooped posture compresses chest.

___ Smokers run lower risk of disease with age.

ACTIVITY 4: RESPIRATORY SYSTEM CROSSWORD

Fill in the crossword below with the words that match these definitions:

ACROSS

1. Tiny air sacs in the lungs.

4. Disease that causes fluid in the lungs.

6. Hair-like appendages in airways.

DOWN

2. The voice box.

3. Lung condition with passages blocked by mucus.

5. Lining of chest cavity.

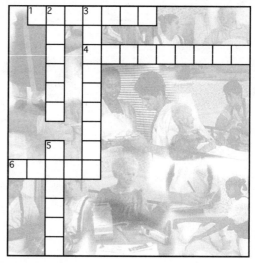

You may use some of the following words:

Atrophy	Diaphragm	Lymph	Pneumonia
Alveoli	Eczema	Osteoporosis	Psoriasis
Bronchi	Emphysema	Pharynx	
Cilia	Larynx	Pleura	

Chapter 16: Anatomy and Physiology: The Endocrine System

 ACTIVITY 1: THE FEMALE ENDOCRINE SYSTEM

Parts of the female endocrine system are indicated below. Write the names of these parts on the lines provided:

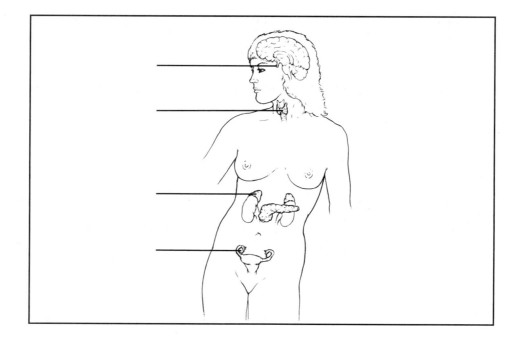

ACTIVITY 2: THE MALE ENDOCRINE SYSTEM

Parts of the male endocrine system are indicated below. Write the names of these parts on the lines provided:

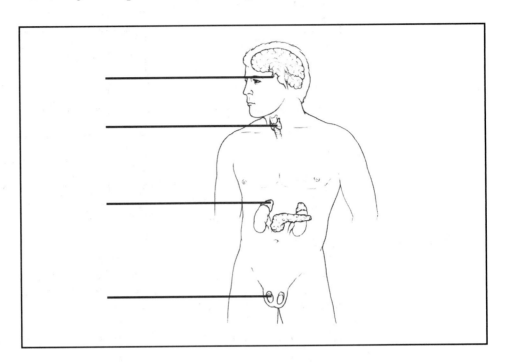

 ## ACTIVITY 3: PITUITARY AND THYROID

By each statement below that is true of the Pituitary, write the letter P. By each statement that is true of the Thyroid, write the letter T. If it is not true of either, write F for false:

___ Located in the throat.

___ Secretes insulin.

___ The master regulator of the body.

___ Responsible for growth.

___ Responsible for sexual development.

___ Regulates calcium.

___ Controls metabolism.

___ Located at the base of the brain.

___ Produces female hormones.

___ The smallest endocrine gland.

✏ ACTIVITY 4: GLANDS

Draw a line from each gland in the left column to a function in the right column:

a. Adrenal   Regulates calcium.

b. Lacrimal   Responsible for growth.

c. Ovary   Regulates other glands.

d. Pancreas   Helps cool the body and eliminate wastes.

e. Parathyroid   Regulates nutrients and electrolyte balance.

f. Pituitary   Releases eggs for reproduction.

g. Thymus   Secretes tears to keep eyes moist.

h. Thyroid   Regulates sugars in the blood.

i. Sweat   Possibly part of the immune system.

✏ ACTIVITY 5: DIABETES

By each statement below that is true of Type I diabetes, write I. By each statement that is true of Type II, write II. If it is not true of either, write F for false. If it is true of both write B:

___ Can be cured with antibiotics.

___ Becomes more common with aging.

___ The body completely lacks insulin.

___ The body has trouble breaking down sugars and starches.

___ Disappears with menopause.

___ Must take injections of insulin.

___ Can sometimes be controlled with diet and exercise.

___ Skin and foot care can be important.

Chapter 17: Anatomy and Physiology: The Sensory System

✏ ACTIVITY 1: THE EYE

Parts of the eye are indicated below. Write the names of these parts on the lines provided:

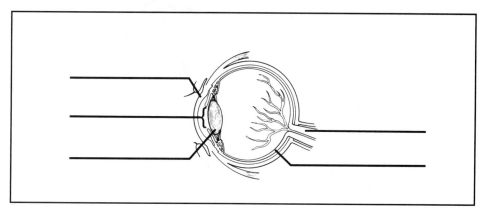

ACTIVITY 2: EYE CHANGES AND DISEASES

Draw a line from each change or disease in the left column to an appropriate definition in the right column:

a. Cataracts   · Difficulty seeing far objects.

b. Glaucoma   Can't see things to the side.

c. Myopia   Pressure build-up inside the eye.

d. Loss of peripheral vision   Difficulty seeing close objects.

e. Presbyopia   Clouding of the lens.

ACTIVITY 3: THE EAR

Parts of the ear are indicated below. Write the names of these parts on the lines provided:

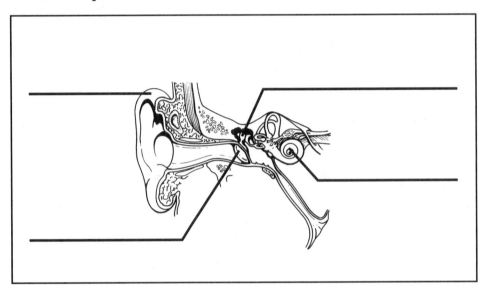

ACTIVITY 4: THE TONGUE

Areas of the tongue are indicated below. On the lines provided, write the names of the tastes that each of these areas is responsible for:

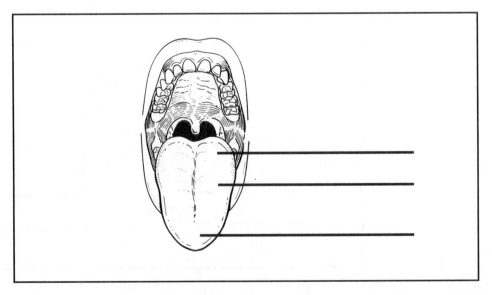

Fill in the blanks with the appropriate word or phrase:

a. The loss of the ability to hear high-pitched sounds is called

_____ .

b. If a person has both myopia and presbyopia, the usual treatment is

_____ .

c. The liquid which fills the eyeball is called _____ .

d. The first taste to decline with aging is usually _____ .

e. The sense of smell _____ with age.

f. The nerve cells that detect touch are located in _____ .

Chapter 18: Anatomy and Physiology: The Digestive System

✏ **ACTIVITY 1: THE DIGESTIVE SYSTEM**

Parts of the digestive system are indicated below. Write the names of these parts on the lines provided:

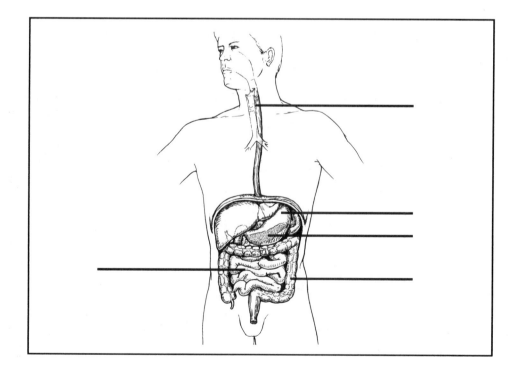

ACTIVITY 2: PARTS OF DIGESTIVE SYSTEM

Draw a line from each part in the left column to a function in the right column:

a. Esophagus

b. Gallbladder

c. Large Intestine

d. Liver

e. Pancreas

f. Small intestine

g. Stomach

h. Teeth

Secretes bile to break down fats.

Grinds up food.

The most important area for digestion.

Mixes food with digestive juices.

Carries food to the stomach.

Makes bile and stores glucose.

Absorbs water from food.

Secretes insulin to help break down starch and sugar.

ACTIVITY 3: AGE-RELATED CHANGES

Check below statements that describe age-related changes of the digestive system:

___ Food is absorbed more slowly.

___ The stomach secretes less gastric juice.

___ Foods taste better.

___ Movement of the esophagus decreases.

___ Movement of the colon decreases.

___ More food is needed.

___ There is a general speeding up of the digestive system.

___ The active ingredients in saliva decrease.

___ The large intestine becomes shorter.

ACTIVITY 4: DIGESTIVE SYSTEM DISORDERS CROSSWORD

Fill in the crossword below with the words that fit the definitions:

ACROSS

4. Cholesterol crystals that form in gallbladder.

5. Buildup of fecal material in large intestine.

DOWN

1. Enlarged blood vessels near rectum.

2. Sac-like inflamed areas in intestine.

3. Loss of tissue or a hole in tissue.

You may use some of the words on the following page:

Atrophy	Enema	Gout	Nausea
Constipation	Emphysema	Hemorrhoids	Pharynx
Digestion	Gallstones	Impaction	Ulcer
Diverticulitis	Gastrointestinal	Liver	

Chapter 19: Anatomy and Physiology: The Nervous System

ACTIVITY 1: THE BRAIN

Parts of the brain are indicated below. Write the names of these parts on the lines provided:

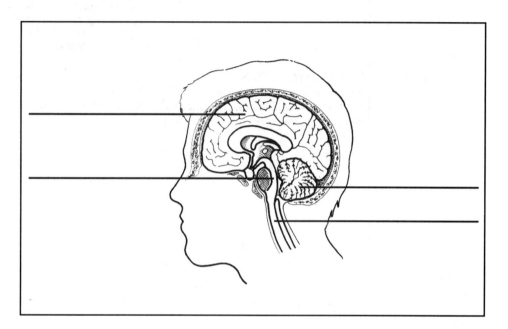

ACTIVITY 2: LOBES

The lobes of the brain are responsible for different functions. Draw line(s) to connect each lobe in the left column with its function(s) in the right column. Note that lobes may have several functions:

a. Frontal lobe

b. Parietal lobe

c. Occipital lobe

d. Temporal lobe

Touch.

Sight.

Temperature change.

Reason.

Pain.

Speech.

Hearing.

Thought.

Pressure.

ACTIVITY 3: THE PERIPHERAL NERVES

Some parts of the peripheral nervous system are indicated below. Write the names of these parts on the lines provided:

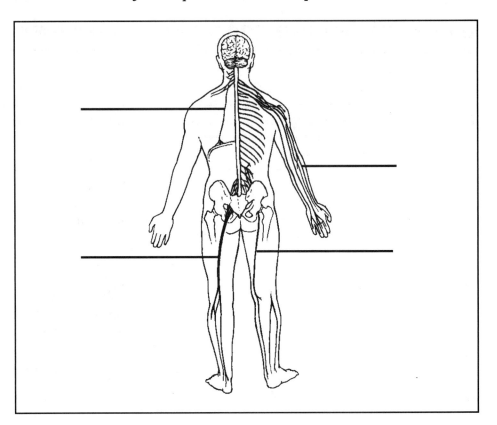

 ## ACTIVITY 4: DISEASES OF THE NERVOUS SYSTEM CROSSWORD

Fill in the crossword below with the nervous system disorders that match these definitions:

ACROSS

1. Mental deterioration.

3. Progressive disease that causes tremors.

4. Large area of the brain stops functioning and there is memory loss.

6. A blood clot in the brain.

DOWN

2. Affected speech.

5. Paralysis on one side.

You may use some of the words on the following page:

Alzheimer   Dementia   Heart attack   Parkinson
Aphasia   Diverticulitis   Impaction   Stroke
Atrophy   Emphysema   Memory   Ulcer
Constipation   Hemiplegia   Nausea

Chapter 20: Infection Control

ACTIVITY 1: INFECTION CONTROL TERMS

Draw a line from each term in the left column to its definition in the right column:

a. Asepsis   Free from all microorganisms.

b. Autoclave   Free from pathogens but not necessarily
                         free of all microorganisms.

c. Clean   Preventing the conditions that allow
                         pathogens to spread.

d. Dirty   A machine that kills microorganisms on
                         objects.

e. Sterile   An object that has been exposed to
                         pathogens.

ACTIVITY 2: SHORT INFECTION CONTROL ANSWERS

Fill in the blanks with the appropriate word or phrase:

a   Specific drugs that kill bacteria are called _____.

b. The body's _____ helps protect us from pathogens.

c. The pathogen _____ causes rheumatic fever.

d. One pathogen called _____ can only survive in living
    cells.

e. Many _____ live on your skin and are not harmful.

ACTIVITY 3: STANDARD PRECAUTIONS

Standard Precautions are measures designed by the CDC to reduce the transmission of microorganisms. Check the substances below that they apply to:

___ Sweat.   ___ Beds.

___ Drinking water.   ___ Handshaking.

___ Mucous membranes.   ___ Nonintact skin.

___ Floor.   ___ Food.

___ All body fluids except sweat.   ___ Human blood.

___ Sterilized medical instruments.

ACTIVITY 4: PERFORMING HAND HYGIENE

Check below the situations in which you should perform hand hygiene:

___ Every five minutes.   ___ After talking to someone.

___ After blowing your nose.   ___ Every time you move more
                                                 than ten feet.
___ Before and after contacting
    every resident.   ___ Before handling food and food
                                                 trays.
___ If one hand touches another.
                                             ___ Any time you feel a chill.
___ After using the bathroom.
                                             ___ After contacting any
___ After contact with soiled linen.   contaminated object.

ACTIVITY 5: PERFORMING HAND HYGIENE PROCEDURE

Below are some of the steps involved in performing hand hygiene. Put them in the order you would perform them. Write the number 1 by the first step, etc:

___ Turn off faucet with a paper   ___ Rinse with warm water with
    towel.   fingers down.

___ Apply soap over hands and   ___ Dry hands with paper towels.
    wrists.
                                          ___ Rub hands together for one
___ Put your hands, fingertips   minute.
    down, under running warm
    water.

Chapter 21: Optimum Level of Health

✎ ACTIVITY 1: TYPES OF NEEDS

To help a resident reach optimum levels of health, you may be providing for four main types of needs. Check these four needs below:

___ Unnecessary needs.   ___ Today's needs.

___ Psychosocial needs.   ___ Physical needs.

___ Spiritual needs.   ___ Your needs.

___ Bizarre needs.   ___ Socialization needs.

___ Optimum needs.

✎ ACTIVITY 2: PHYSICAL NEEDS

You will be helping residents fulfill their physical needs. Check the needs below that represent physical needs:

___ Food.   ___ Respect.   ___ Books.

___ Affection.   ___ Information.   ___ Medications.

___ Exercise.   ___ Medical care.   ___ Feeling worthwhile.

___ Cleanliness.   ___ Rest.

✎ ACTIVITY 3: SOCIALIZATION GRID

Find and circle five words in the grid below that represent socialization needs:

WORD LIST

INFORMATION

IDEAS

SUPPORT

AFFECTION

STIMULATION

```
I X H H W K B Q E F I D K N B
S P E L T E H Y A D E Q O Q I
R N E A F F E C T I O N Q T N
I W I P V S I V J I O A T G F
P D C U R U B W L Y P W L K O
P I E R A P F A W L R L L N R
W O Y A K P I S E A S W Q Y M
X S D K S O X Q Q W F E U B A
E U F O J R P C W A W C E O T
O Q V P J T F J Q D S A F K I
C E B J E O P R N U B D B U O
X G O M N M U V O R W R Y Z N
V D M K S N M L K Y V L W V B
V Z S T I M U L A T I O N Q B
W F U D X P M N W C Y E A U A
```

Chapter 22: Age-Specific Issues

ACTIVITY 1: PUBERTY ISSUES

Check below issues that commonly affect young people at the age of puberty:

___ Body image.   ___ Menstruation.

___ Dementia.   ___ Distance from parents.

___ Love and sexuality.   ___ Cataracts.

___ Arteriosclerosis.   ___ Masturbation.

___ Stroke.

ACTIVITY 2: DISEASES OF AGING, PART 1

Draw a line from each common disease of aging in the left column to a definition in the right column:

a. Arteriosclerosis   Clouding of the lens of the eye.

b. Cataracts   Enlarged blood vessels around rectum.

c. Diabetes   Hardening of the arteries.

d. Parkinson's   Swollen and painful blood vessels.

e. Varicose Veins   Progressive disease that causes tremors.

f. Hemorrhoids   Disease that makes it hard to use carbohydrates.

ACTIVITY 3: DISEASES OF AGING, PART 2

Draw a line from each common disease of aging in the left column to a definition in the right column:

a. Congestive heart failure   A blood clot in the brain.

b. Hypertension   Inability of the heart to pump enough blood.

c. Prostate disease   High blood pressure.

d. Pressure sores   Swelling of a gland that surrounds the urethra in men.

e. Stroke   Skin that reddens and breaks open from continuous pressure.

ACTIVITY 4: AGE-SPECIFIC CROSSWORD

Fill in the crossword below with the words that fit the definitions:

ACROSS

2. Inability of the body to use carbohydrates.

6. Monthly loss of blood of women of sexual age.

7. The beginning age of sexual maturation.

DOWN

1. A decrease in size and strength of bones.

2. Loss of mental capacity.

3. Tiny mites that infest the skin.

4. A hormone needed to turn carbohydrates into energy.

5. Sugars and starches that supply quick energy.

You may use some of the following words:

Adrenalin	Carbohydrates	Insulin	Pressure Sores
Aphasia	Dementia	Menstruation	Puberty
Arteriosclerosis	Diabetes	Osteoarthritis	Scabies
Cataracts	Gastritis	Osteoporosis	Sexual
Constipation	Hemorrhoids	Parkinson's	Stroke

Chapter 23: Communicating with the Residents

ACTIVITY 1: NON-VERBAL COMMUNICATION

Check below examples of non-verbal communication:

___ Rigid posture.   ___ Clenched teeth.   ___ Winking.

___ Talking softly.   ___ Shouting.   ___ Hugging.

___ Writing a note.   ___ Tapping your foot.   ___ Sarcasm.

___ Tight facial expression.   ___ Pointing to words in a book.

ACTIVITY 2: COMMUNICATION SKILLS

Check below examples of good communication skills:

___ Explaining a procedure before you do it.

___ Looking away when someone is talking to you.

___ Interrupting to hurry someone who is very slow.

___ Speaking in a friendly voice.

___ Using baby talk with an older resident.

___ Cursing someone who is angry with you.

___ Speaking slowly and clearly to someone confused.

___ Stop explaining procedures to residents who are confused.

___ Acting interested.

___ Folding your arms and talking with a severe expression.

ACTIVITY 3: COMMUNICATION GRID

In the following letter grid, find and circle six words or phrases that indicate possible barriers to communication:

WORD LIST

APHASIA

ANGER

IMPAIRED HEARING

BLINDNESS

FOREIGN LANGUAGE

CONFUSION

```
P F W S F F R J J S E F C K C H C O
G O J T U L B J B V X I R P X N O L
S R F A P H A S I A C N O W S G N M
Q E L R V B T T B K X A U S N M F K
P I W A S Q M Y F T V Q E I E M U K
E G H G Z O L O D B M N R O U N S I
V N R N W T Z I Y C D A I O P F I T
K L D I O Q D R D N E Y N R E B O F
S A F Y B V F I I H W L V N V S N A
Y N D F H M B L D R S D X T K N U I
O G V B Z F B E V H I T P E C P P D
A U W P K H R Y X D L B L F B W P X
K A W X M I H K W H E V B D W X S Y
W G M R A P M B Y X Y A N G E R V E
B E G P F Z Z F E O I N A G P C X C
S I M B L F Q P G K G L G K D V P D
L I R A A E R B I G Q P O G F V T L
S H E N D S V P U W W O A I N G L Z
```

Chapter 24: Principles of Observation

ACTIVITY 1: NURSING ASSISTANT OBSERVATIONS

The nursing assistant often has more contact with a resident than anyone else. Check below information that a nursing assistant is responsible for gathering and reporting:

___ Interpreting blood tests.

___ IV fluid rate.

___ General responsiveness.

___ What other residents say about the resident's behavior.

___ If resident is oriented.

___ Intake and output.

___ Medication response.

___ Stomach contents.

___ Unusual symptoms or behavior.

___ Activity level.

ACTIVITY 2: TYPES OF OBSERVATIONS

By each of the observations below, write the word that describes which sense you would most likely use to make that observation: see, hear, smell, or touch:

_____ Reddened area of skin.

_____ Confused speech.

_____ Cloudy eyes.

_____ Damp skin.

_____ Description of a new pain.

_____ New odor in urine.

_____ Uneaten food.

_____ Strong breath.

_____ Wheezing.

_____ Nervous shudders.

_____ Odor from a cast.

_____ Uncombed hair.

_____ Hot sensitive area of skin.

ACTIVITY 3: REPORTING OBSERVATIONS

Check below the information that you should report if you make any unusual observation:

___ Name of resident.

___ What you observed.

___ Room and bed number.

___ How you were feeling when you made the observation.

___ Time of observation.

___ What other residents say about the observation.

___ Your opinion of what the observation means.

___ Your own home address.

Chapter 25: Measuring Weight and Height

ACTIVITY 1: ACCURATE WEIGHING

Check below the techniques that will help you obtain accurate weight measurements:

___ Always weigh the resident in different clothing.

___ Always weigh the resident at the same time of day.

___ Always weigh the resident right after eating.

___ Have the resident empty his or her bladder before weighing.

___ Keep the scales in one place if you can.

___ Have the resident wear as much clothing as possible.

___ If the resident has a cast or brace, subtract its approximate weight.

___ Always check the scales by weighing yourself first.

___ Always use the same scales.

___ Always push the weights to zero with scale empty and check it for proper balance.

ACTIVITY 2: WEIGHING PROCEDURE

Below are some of the steps involved in weighing a resident. Put them in the order you would perform them. Write the number 1 by the first step, etc:

___ Adjust the weights and read the weight.

___ Assist the resident off the scale.

___ Assist the resident on the scale.

___ Check the scale for proper balance.

___ Explain what you are going to do, and perform hand hygiene.

___ Put a gait belt on the resident.

___ Record the weight.

___ Take the resident to the scale.

___ Return the weights to zero.

ACTIVITY 3: TYPES OF SCALES

*The type of scale in the photo below is called a _____.
Check the correct answer below:*

___ Standing balance scale.

___ Bathroom scale.

___ Wheelchair scale.

___ Mechanical lift scale.

___ Sliding scale.

___ Digital scale.

ACTIVITY 4: PROCEDURE FOR MEASURING HEIGHT IN BED

Below are some of the steps involved in measuring the height of a resident who cannot stand. Put them in the order you would perform them. Write the number 1 by the first step, etc:

___ Position the resident flat and straight in bed.

___ Mark the heels and head on the sheet.

___ Roll the resident away and measure the distance between the marks with a tape measure.

___ Record the height.

___ Explain what you will be doing and perform hand hygiene.

___ Write down the measurement and roll the resident back.

ACTIVITY 5: MEASURING HEIGHT WITH CONTRACTURES

Residents with contractures cannot lie straight. You must measure the height in segments and then add them together. On the drawing below, mark lines to show the top and bottom of each segment you would measure:

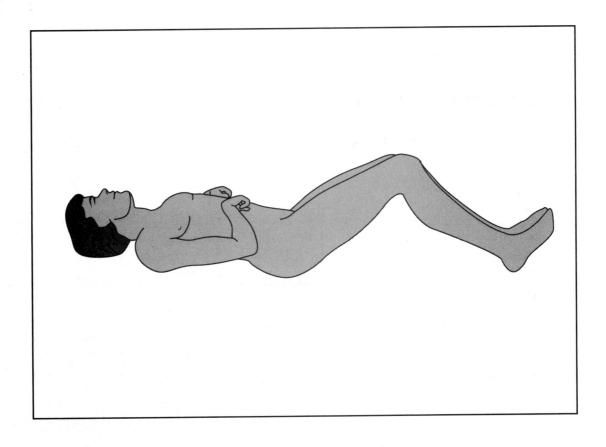

Chapter 26: Measuring Vital Signs

 ACTIVITY 1: VITAL SIGNS GRID

Find and circle the four vital signs on this letter grid:

WORD LIST

BLOOD PRESSURE
TEMPERATURE
PULSE
RESPIRATION

```
N L S T N P K S R U C C R C W M X B T J
I C F X L J T O G D B V V U G X P P E A
G J S I R J C A F B A F J K R A S X M P
R R E D C I L Y G S T V E L V M K D P L
C J F I N J F U U Q P T S D G U M T E I
S R R P N C G B X D T Q G V W F E O R G
M Z E F H P L W Z K O U P K Y R C T A R
C F S L O P U L S E S D S Z U O I R T K
N T P C N J V E R D U O H S Z H U H U W
J P I Y Z Q O E X C K H S R Q A T U R F
J G R P X R T Q Z I T E Z E V O J U E W
K O A H J Q P M Z A R F E E X G L J K F
Z D T V L H D G N P L O Q K U Q U X L I
Y H I B A E T D D R A S W D T L T Y K N
I E O C N Z U O C L V B P F I C J L P U
A R N D S P O S S H V O X U T I G K M R
Y M L H F L T L I F F E M X B S I A M H
D K J N B V O M P M Z J L I J Z E P C Q
W B L V U F L H G Q J I L Q A W T U A Q
A Z R Z H I R Z Q E M T G I U V H D D H
```

 ACTIVITY 2: TYPES OF THERMOMETERS

Write the type of thermometer indicated in each blank space:

A. _____

B. _____

C. _____

D. _____

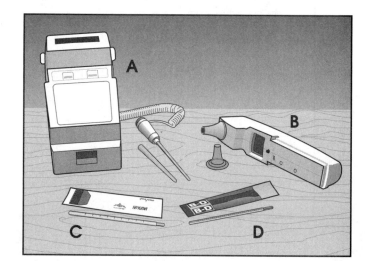

ACTIVITY 3: READING A GLASS THERMOMETER

In the blank space below each glass thermometer below, write the temperature indicated:

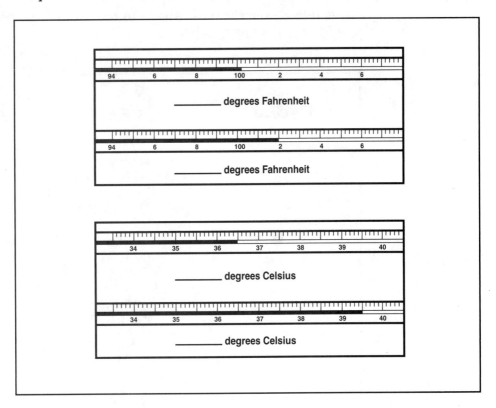

_____ degrees Fahrenheit

_____ degrees Fahrenheit

_____ degrees Celsius

_____ degrees Celsius

ACTIVITY 4: NORMAL READINGS

Write the appropriate normal readings in the blank spaces below:

Normal Fahrenheit temperature for an oral thermometer is _____F.

Normal Celsius temperature for a rectal thermometer is _____C.

Normal Fahrenheit temperature for an axillary thermometer is _____F.

ACTIVITY 5: TAKING THE PULSE

Draw a line from the word Radial to the spot on the body where you would take the radial pulse:

Draw a line from the word Apical to the spot on the body where you would take the apical pulse:

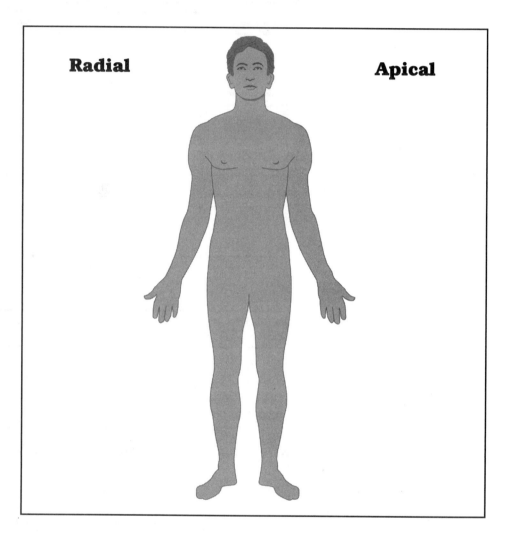

Radial   **Apical**

 ## ACTIVITY 6: TAKING AN ACCURATE BLOOD PRESSURE

Check below any techniques that will help you take an accurate and consistent blood pressure:

___ Always have the resident exercise first.

___ Always have the resident in the same position.

___ For an obese resident, use a child's pressure cuff.

___ Change arms for every reading.

___ Check the stethoscope to be sure it is functioning.

___ Take the blood pressure in a quiet area, away from distractions.

___ If the resident has an IV, take the blood pressure on the arm with the IV.

___ Do not apply the cuff over clothing.

___ If the reading seems unusual, repeat the procedure.

ACTIVITY 7: COUNTING RESPIRATIONS

While counting respirations, there are a number of observations you should make that can have a direct bearing on respiration. Check these observations below:

___ Eye color.

___ Rate of respirations.

___ Clothing size.

___ Color of skin.

___ Condition of shoes.

___ Amount of gray hair.

___ Character of breathing.

___ Rhythm of breathing.

___ Eye blinking.

ACTIVITY 8: VITAL SIGNS CROSSWORD

Fill in the crossword below with the vital signs terms that match these definitions:

ACROSS

2. Measured over the heart.

4. Blood pressure when the heart is contracting.

5. Measured in the ear.

6. The first recording of vital signs when someone enters a facility.

DOWN

1. Blood pressure when the heart is relaxed.

3. Metric measure of temperature.

7. Relating to the armpit.

You may use some of the following words:

Aphasia	Brachial	Expiration	Pressure
Apical	Celsius	Fahrenheit	Stethoscope
Axillary	Centigrade	Gastritis	Systolic
Baseline	Constipation	Inspiration	Tympanic
Basetype	Diastolic	Osteoporosis	

Chapter 27: The "Fifth Vital Sign" — Pain

ACTIVITY 1: RECOGNIZING PAIN

Check below the three main things you need to report about pain:

___ Its intensity.

___ Its speed.

___ The time it stops.

___ Its nature.

___ Its name.

___ Its location.

___ Its moderation.

ACTIVITY 2: PAIN SCALES

On the three scales shown below, place a check on the place that would indicate the most severe pain

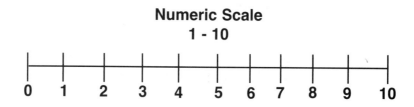

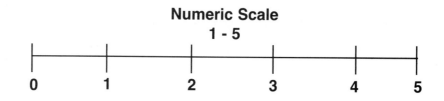

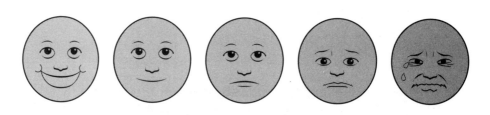

ACTIVITY 3: THE NATURE OF PAIN

Check below on the likely questions you could use to help you report the nature of a pain.

___ "Do you feel any pain?"

___ "Is it worse than Mr. Smith's pain?"

___ "Does it feel like a burning?"

___ "Did you feel this pain when you were a child?"

___ "Does it feel like a pinching?"

___ "When did the pain start?"

___ "Does it feel like a stabbing?"

___ "Can you point to somewhere in the room that is like your pain?"

ACTIVITY 4: PAIN

Find and circle in the grid below seven words that refer to pain.

WORD LIST

INTENSITY

LOCATION

NATURE

BURNING

PINCHING

STABBING

CHRONIC

```
D Y A Z K S T A B B I N G L Y F W L
E X L N Y B H A G Q I Z K Q Q K B I
G I T R L W F N N R J Z S Q Q C N Z
F N Z R I O K B I P P A P V U H F U
S T C S U S S R N T I Y Z W H J Y N
I E W O N M W K R E N Y S K J Z Q A
O N V E P R P Y U Q C Q I Z B P O T
W S U B B R F P B S H R V D A V T U
S I B M M M L I R I I H U J B J Y R
H T C D U I Q J H A N K N T A E J E
J Y W H H N V N E N G O J C G D G V
G B C G R V O U V W G C K P X C L V
Q L T U Z O R I C O O Y H A B L Z O
T X V B E A N N T T Y C L Z A F K U
E G J N L N L I G A P O C M P C Y K
I L P R X Q Y E C Y C B Q E L M G N
O A S L U Y W C K B X O P M M Z Z A
N N B N E B V C M O O A L Y K S Z Q
```

Chapter 28: Activities of Daily Living

 ## ACTIVITY 1: CONDITIONS THAT LIMIT INDEPENDENCE

Find and circle in this letter grid six medical conditions that are likely to limit a person's ability to perform the activities of daily living:

WORD LIST

MULTIPLE SCLEROSIS

CEREBRAL PALSY

ARTHRITIS

PARKINSONS DISEASE

STROKE

PARALYSIS

```
D M P L T L V A D R C N F M L D P N V E P
A G H F J F V M L P L Y A A G G D U Y T W
P R P M X J A C U K L R O A B U L L F I G
A N T E Z I A F T R C S H T P E H K D J E
R B S H C E R E B R A L P A L S Y W N S A
K I L M R L I T S X Z M M S T W G K W G D
I M J U L I U X G A A D S F L S O O J F H
N J T E V Q T D Y C T Y T F A H F I H N Y
S U V H U K T I V D F O R S N D V R A O H
O G J X O R G A S I I P X X T T B G D M X
N T A P W E P Y O C M Z D S N R F M A L M
S E S X J R N U I P I B D J V B O U E B D
D K Y O G Z J Y J V A U H V L K S K Z O Y
I F H P C K Q K C U F Z U O U P O R E T D
S X X P A R A L Y S I S W N E C L B B A Y
E M T B C J K F D W K L W C A N A W S F Y
A E L B X N E U M J T U E N S P X P Q G J
S S U S K H A D K X C G P G R Q E U D F Z
E O L M U L T I P L E S C L E R O S I S L
Q W H B S F G L I Q F Q A V Z X J A T F G
S X W C E L X O F F F Y Z E G A N N E I D
```

The New Nursing Assistant Workbook and Skills Checklists ———————————————— 49

ACTIVITY 2: LIMITED PHYSICAL STRENGTH AND ABILITY

Check below the recommended techniques that will help you assist a person with limited physical strength and abilities:

___ Break a task into smaller tasks.

___ Encouraging the resident to say in bed and rest.

___ Help them get used to the fact that they cannot do certain things.

___ Have them do as much of a task as they can.

___ Encourage walking if the resident is able.

___ Do a task yourself if you can do it faster.

___ Encourage independence.

___ Make a joke of any task performed badly.

ACTIVITY 3: EATING

Check below recommended implements to assist a person with limited abilities at eating:

___ Cups with very small handles.

___ Non-skid dishes.

___ Very heavy cutlery.

___ Knives, spoons and forks with big handles or ridged handles.

___ Flat plates with no lip.

___ Spill-proof cups.

___ Baby bottles.

___ Knives, spoons and forks with angled ends.

___ Small plastic disposable cutlery.

___ Knives, spoons and forks that clip onto a person's hands.

___ Chopsticks.

ACTIVITY 4: DRESSING

Check below recommended special items to assist a person with limited abilities at dressing:

___ Zippers with tiny handles.

___ Buttonhooks.

___ Very tight clothing.

___ Not wearing any clothing.

___ Clothing with front closures.

___ Unusual hooks.

___ Velcro closures.

___ Roomy pullover clothing.

___ Clothing with many tiny buttons.

___ Long handled shoe-horn.

Write short answers in the blanks below:

a. Residents who feel they can no longer do anything for themselves are displaying _____.

b. Muscles become weak without _____.

c. Write below three common activities of daily living:

_____

_____

_____

Chapter 29: Resident Activity Needs

ACTIVITY 1: ACTIVITIES FOR RESIDENTS WHO CAN AMBULATE

Check below the recommended ways you can encourage activities for residents who can ambulate:

___ Force the resident to try new things.

___ Help the resident be groomed and ready for an activity.

___ Keep the resident informed of the time and place of events.

___ Encourage them to do things too difficult for them.

___ Assist the resident getting to and from the activity.

___ Show an interest in their activities.

___ Spring new activities on the resident as a surprise.

___ Keep them in bed.

ACTIVITY 2: RESIDENTS CONFINED TO BED

Write below three recreational activities you can recommend for residents confined to bed:

_____

_____

_____

Activity 3: Confused Residents

Write below three recreational activities you can recommend for confused residents:

_____

_____

_____

Chapter 30: Physical Needs of the Resident

Activity 1: Physical Needs Grid

Find and circle in this letter grid five words that describe physical needs:

WORD LIST

SLEEP
EXERCISE
FOOD
ELIMINATION
CLEANLINESS

```
N N M R W K D Q Q Q S D O I K H S K
C L E A N L I N E S S H U M E B U R
V O L S B G K R H S Q B M S G J X O
E H Q J D V P R A S Q P I K Y N G O
H M X G W Z V G Q S C C W Y R V B T
T K J F Q V V J X X R U U S N Q T U
D E U X K L S A Z E E A R B N G G I
J Z L R R D F U X R A V A H S D Z T
Q Z Y I H G M E W L H D O V P E D I
U T O C M L O Y Z D F K F O O D K B
Y I I U W I Q Q Q V F V Q T A R H N
M T D D M G N U T A R M M X X V L V
Y A Z I O I I A P W S H K S E G R M
O M X E N T I B T D B I E I V S I K
I R E G N V M M G I D B Q Q F W M Y
S L E E P R B I S B O J I Z O C C S
Y X Z Y C Q U Z R L D N H E Z A I X
T D L M N Z M Q M E U T S C Q A Y S
```

ACTIVITY 2: SLEEP

Check below recommended ways you can assist residents in sleeping:

___ Encourage the resident to sleep at different times every day.

___ Provide regular periods of quiet, uninterrupted time.

___ Play loud music.

___ Provide a light cover during naps.

___ Make the resident comfortable.

___ Recommend strong medications.

___ Remove the shoes and loosen belts during rest.

___ Encourage eating immediately before bedtime.

___ Discourage exercise.

___ Keep the bed neat and unwrinkled.

ACTIVITY 3: SHORT ANSWERS

Write short answers in the blanks below:

a. _____ is one of the best exercises.

b. If a resident cannot leave bed, another form of exercise is

_____.

c. The body temperature becomes _____ during sleep.

d. Assisting a resident to walk is called _____.

Chapter 31: Resident Belongings and Prostheses

ACTIVITY 1: EYEGLASSES

Check below recommended ways to help take care of eyeglasses:

___ Discourage using eyeglasses for reading.

___ Wash eyeglasses under running water.

___ Have the resident sleep in the eyeglasses.

___ Dry eyeglasses with a stiff paper towel.

___ While cleaning eyeglasses, check for damage.

___ Report any damage to the charge nurse.

___ Eyeglasses should never be placed in their case.

___ Place a cloth in the bottom of the sink while washing eyeglasses.

ACTIVITY 2: ARTIFICIAL LIMB

Check below recommended ways to help a resident with an artificial limb:

___ Protect the stump with a stump sock.

___ Check the artificial limb regularly for damage.

___ Have the resident use the limb only on special occasions.

___ Check the stump regularly for swelling.

___ Report any damage to the charge nurse.

___ Check the stump for redness or swelling.

ACTIVITY 3: PERSONAL BELONGINGS GRID

Find and circle in this letter grid seven words or phrases that describe likely personal belongings of a resident:

WORD LIST

CLOTHING

TOILET ARTICLES

AMBULATION DEVICES

APPLIANCES

TELEVISIONS

RADIOS

PROSTHESES

```
R L Z G F B H P M S U V N D Y F S M I H V N S S
R P E S U C S U P R O S T H E S E S P O H J X J
C P J W M O H S X F O S J N E X D S A U X O O G
C Y P Y N S A D T K T R C A O A I W G S P C N Z
E N D K B K M K X O H N J S Z E F E X M Y I M W
O Q R T P D B M Z L I H S E L M C E P S H P T F
C H I E B U U D L D N L N N K E R E R T S V D X
O Z Z Q P Z L X I G Y F E G Z P W T O L H L F Y
R F V V Q B A T M T S N B T N C O L B T T F G T
L K U T L F T C G N T Q A S A V C I Y K Y L N G
O B X S E S I L X L D K J S A R I K R V Z N Q P
N J C W V E O M B U X T W K T T T B Q K G C R S
C J V F L E N O B I W G X U F I I I N B N F A L
U T V A X T D A S J W B N C W S W N C O B R H Z
Y E V U L M E S L C H K Z C P Q T E Y L S O B H
E K C X J Q V H H N U R A D I O S O B P E P B V
A M F I B D I U C R H N P T T H E P O R U S A E
W X M X R A C V N F L O E E Z U P X D H R C S M
X F A Y A R E S Y I R G B H W S L F I C F S V D
T L D G I N S C U B B B M H O J X R X J Z C Q E
U I K U H O C M C I S R L E J Q T B V M H M V V
T E L E V I S I O N S E R T W T W D R A E X Z V
R R T U D J T X C K R A P P L I A N C E S B N L
Y H U Z L F O A J A H A D Q W K M G Q X G W G A
```

ACTIVITY 4: VALUABLE BELONGINGS

Write short answers in the blanks below:

a. Expensive items should be taken home by the family or kept in

_____.

b. Small expensive items should be kept in an envelope marked with

the _____, _____, and

_____.

c. Items locked up or taken home by the family should be

_____.

ACTIVITY 5: HEARING AID

Check below recommended ways to help take care of hearing aids:

___ Store a hearing aid in the safe when not in use.

___ Report the need for new batteries to the charge nurse.

___ When not in use, it should be turned off.

___ Encourage the resident to bathe in the hearing aid.

___ Test the hearing aid in your own ear.

___ Keep the hearing aid away from moisture or heat.

___ Check the resident's ear regularly for wax build-up.

___ Shout into the hearing aid to test it.

___ When not in use store it properly in a marked container.

Chapter 32: The Environment of Care: Resident Safety

ACTIVITY 1: SPECIAL RISKS

Check below any conditions that may increase the safety risk for a long-term care resident.

___ Hearing problems.

___ Sleeping.

___ Dementia.

___ General weakness.

___ Overeating.

___ Vision problems.

___ Socializing.

___ Medications that cause drowsiness.

ACTIVITY 2: SAFETY INSPECTION

Write a plus sign (+) before the items below that would increase patient safety. Write a minus sign (-) before items that would endanger a patient's safety.

___ Well-lit corridor.

___ Loose carpet on floor.

___ Object on floor.

___ Grab bars.

___ Slippers left on floor.

___ Floppy shoes.

___ Call switch in reach.

___ Burned out light bulb.

___ Elevated toilet seat.

___ Worn electrical cord.

ACTIVITY 3: FIRE EXTINGUISHERS

Before each type of fire, write the type of fire extinguisher that is designed to put out that fire--A, B or C.

___ Burning paper.   ___ Bedside lamp on fire.

___ Electrical device on fire   ___ Burning oil.

___ Burning grease   ___ Burning Cloth

___ Burning wood.

ACTIVITY 4: RACE

The memory-word RACE is to help you remember what to do in case of a fire. Draw a line to connect each letter below to the appropriate action to remember.

a. **R**   Run out of the building.
                       Rescue residents near the fire.
                       Research location of all fire extinguishers.

b. **A**   Ambulate bedridden patients.
                       Avoid the area of the fire.
                       Activate the alarm.

c. **C**   Contain the fire by closing doors.
                       Call for help.
                       Crush any matches.

d. **E**   Evacuate the building.
                       Extinguish the fire if it is small.
                       End any rescue operations.

Fill in the crossword below with the vital signs terms that match these definitions:

ACROSS

3. A device to put out a fire.

4. A common accident that causes many deaths a year in older people.

5. The loss of clear thinking.

DOWN

1. Any safety danger.

2. A gas that can increase the danger of fire.

6. The area around a resident.

7. A device to call automatically for assistance.

You may use some of the following words:

Alarm	Disaster	Fire	Oxygen
Alzheimer's	Fall	Hazard	Restraints
Blanket	Environment	Nitrogen	Telephone
Corridor	Epidemic	Nozzle	
Dementia	Extinguisher		

Chapter 33: Moving a Resident

✎ ACTIVITY 1: BODY MECHANICS

Check below the recommended ways to protect yourself while lifting a resident or other heavy weight:

___ Bend forward at the waist and lift with your back muscles.

___ Get as close as you can to the weight.

___ Use your legs as much as possible.

___ Spread your feet as far as possible.

___ Wear a support belt.

___ Be sure to twist your back as you lift.

___ If a weight is too heavy for you, get help.

___ Always lift; never push, pull or roll.

___ Put a gait belt on the resident.

___ Take short steps.

✎ ACTIVITY 2: MOVING A RESIDENT UP IN BED

Below are some of the steps involved in moving a resident up in bed. Put them in the order you would perform them. Write the number 1 by the first step, etc:

___ On a count of three, have the resident push toward the head of the bed as you lift and move him.

___ Place a pillow against the headboard to protect the resident's head.

___ If the resident can help, have him bend the knees and brace his feet against the mattress.

___ Perform hand hygiene and explain what you are doing.

___ Place your hands under the resident's buttocks and shoulders.

___ Position yourself next to the bed with your feet 12 inches apart.

ACTIVITY 3: TURNING A RESIDENT TOWARD YOU

Below are some of the steps involved in turning a resident toward you. Put them in the order you would perform them. Write the number 1 by the first step, etc:

___ Roll the resident toward you.

___ Cross the resident's arms over his chest.

___ Perform hand hygiene and explain what you will be doing.

___ Support the resident's back in this position with a pillow.

___ Cross the leg farthest from you over the leg closest to you.

___ Reach across the resident and put a hand behind his shoulder, and place your other hand on the resident's hip.

ACTIVITY 4: COMPLETING A MOVE

Check below the activities you should perform after completing any transfer or repositioning:

___ Leave the bed in its lowest position.

___ Wash the resident's hands.

___ Turn out the lights.

___ Make sure the call bell is within the resident's reach.

___ Perform hand hygiene.

___ Leave the bed in its highest position.

___ Thank the resident for cooperating.

___ Make sure the side rails are up.

___ Change the resident's position again.

ACTIVITY 5: SHORT ANSWERS

Write short answers in the blanks below:

a. To use a mechanical lift, there should be _____ healthcare workers.

b. To transfer a dependent resident, there should be _____ healthcare workers.

c. To move a partially paralyzed resident, position the wheelchair on the resident's _____ side.

d. In transferring a dependent resident, the wheelchair should be positioned at a _____ angle.

e. Make sure a resident who cannot move himself is in correct body _____.

✏ ACTIVITY 6: REPOSITIONING CROSSWORD

Fill in the crossword below with the words that fit the definitions:

ACROSS

2. Alignment of the skeletal body.

3. A belt placed on the resident to help in a move.

4. A belt placed on the healthcare worker to help prevent injury.

6. The area on which an object rests.

DOWN

1. Place where the weight of an object is focused.

5. A folded bedsheet under the resident from shoulders to knees.

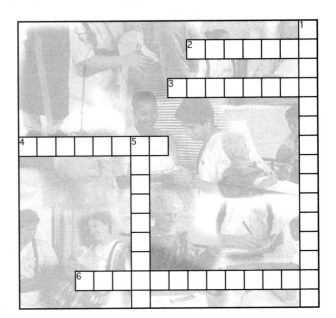

You may use some of the following words:

Axis of symmetry	Centrum	Gatorade	Open end
Apical point	Center of gravity	Half sheet	Posture
Baseline	Charted node	Lift belt	Prosthesis
Basetype	Focus of weight	Lift sheet	Space weight
Base of support	Gait belt	Lift machine	Tear sheet

Chapter 34: Ambulation

✏ ACTIVITY 1: BENEFITS OF AMBULATION

Check below eight statements that are benefits of ambulation:

___ Strengthens muscles.

___ Improves self-esteem.

___ Improves circulation.

___ Lowers body temperature.

___ Provides independence.

___ Relieves pressure on other body parts.

___ Prevents stroke.

___ Helps urinary and bowel systems.

___ Moves joints.

___ Relieves pressure on other body parts.

✏ ACTIVITY 2: SAFETY OF AMBULATION

Check below the things a resident must be able to do in order to ambulate safely:

___ Leap at least ten inches off the ground.

___ Maintain sitting balance unassisted.

___ Rise unassisted from a full squat.

___ Stand up.

___ Stand on one leg unassisted.

___ Maintain standing balance.

___ Talk coherently.

___ Run a mile.

✏ ACTIVITY 3: ASSISTING AMBULATION PROCEDURES

Below are some of the steps involved in helping a resident who is in bed, stand up to assist with ambulation. Put them in the order you would perform them. Write the number 1 by the first step, etc:

___ Stand on the resident's stronger side.

___ Fasten a gait belt around the resident's waist and help the resident put on firm shoes.

___ Allow time for the resident to gain balance before walking.

___ Perform hand hygiene, explain what you will be doing, and what you expect the resident to do.

___ Grip both sides of the gait belt and help the resident up.

___ Assist the resident to a sitting position.

✏ ACTIVITY 4: AMBULATION CROSSWORD

Fill in the crossword below with the words that fit the definitions:

ACROSS

1. A straight support device with four rubber tips.

3. A frame worn on leg or back to limit movement or assist movement.

5. A portable support frame with wheels on two or more legs.

DOWN

2. Helping someone walk.

4. A portable support frame without wheels.

You may use some of the following words:

Axis of symmetry	Base	Gait belt	Pick up walker
Activation	Brace	Jumper seat	Quad cane
Ambulation	Center of gravity	Lift machine	Rolling walker
	Device		

Chapter 35: Safety in Ambulation and Restraint

✏ ACTIVITY 1: ID BRACELET

Check below three types of information that you would NOT expect to find on a resident's ID bracelet:

___ Name.

___ Medications being taken.

___ Room and bed number.

___ Current Diseases.

___ Age.

___ Sex.

___ Doctor's name.

___ Social Security Number.

___ Any allergies.

✏ ACTIVITY 2: SIDE RAILS

Check below five rules that apply to the safe use of side rails:

___ Use padding for residents who thrash about in bed.

___ Side rails are to be removed completely for many procedures.

___ Restraints are never tied to the rails.

___ Always leave the rails down during the day for everyone.

___ Always lock the rails in place, either up or down.

___ Before raising or lowering, make sure the resident's arms and legs are out of the way.

___ Broken rails should be reported immediately.

___ Teach the resident how to lock and move the rails.

✏ ACTIVITY 3: WHEELCHAIRS

Check below six rules that apply to the safe use of wheelchairs:

___ When moving a resident in a wheelchair, be alert for hazards.

___ Keep the resident's clothing away from the wheels.

___ Always lock the brakes when trying to move the wheelchair.

___ Report broken or defective parts immediately.

___ Teach the resident how to crawl up into a wheelchair from a fallen position.

___ Always lock the brakes when transferring a resident into a wheelchair.

___ Have the footrests up when transferring a resident into the chair.

___ Have the footrests up when moving a resident out into the hallway.

___ Use extra care in transfers into a wheelchair for those with fragile skin.

✏ ACTIVITY 4: RESTRAINTS

Check below seven rules that apply to the safe and legal use of restraints:

___ Use restraints only if the bed or chair has wheels.

___ Restraints are only used if there is a physician's order.

___ Restraints are used sometimes as punishment for uncooperative residents.

___ The resident must be able to reach a call button.

___ A resident in supportive restraints must be checked often.

___ Restraints can be used for a short period if the staff is very busy.

___ Restraints should fit snugly, without binding.

___ Restraints are to be tied in place with simple slip knots.

___ Restraints must be released regularly to allow for massage and exercise.

___ Restraints must not restrict circulation.

✏ ACTIVITY 5: RESTRAINT GRID

Find and circle in this letter grid five words or phrases that describe types of restraints:

WORD LIST

CLOTHING
VEST SUPPORT
PELVIC SUPPORT
MITTENS
LIMB TIES

```
X C L O T H I N G G R B C D M Q B J  Q I
E V L R P B R U C X H P J Y W H Y G O Q
B T L I L I J L I P U I Z N X Y T P K D
C F E P M H V X A K J N C P A R O U M D
B V N Q I B D N M G A I J Z O B O Q Z S
S J J Q K L T J Y Z U K J P Q U A F V O
V M J D Z L O I Q K V H P M N I A Z D H
G J Q R W X K M E K K U P X P V L N E P
M P T W I L G A D S S K J D S A W F E D
F J V W P O E U W C B B E X C Q Z O K A
V C R F P Z V N I Y A X F S N N D M J W
H R R F S M X V K O K P K O R H E L X T
M J T P J Y L Y F U Z T P B S T E H F O
N P A P I E R J H G B X B K M O C P U G
W P F F P T U F V E S T S U P P O R T P
B N Z P C T Q Z J X Y A D S I U V X L P
E E K Q T D I X D D Z P K V P D V M C I
Y I C W C P O K X U Y S F P W T A X S N
M K M I T T E N S U E A I L N E J O A A
Y Z A O N J E J R K L J G H N J S T N R
```

Chapter 36: Inactivity and Range of Motion Exercises

 ACTIVITY 1: RANGE OF MOTION TERMS

Draw a line between each term in the left column and the appropriate definition in the right column:

a.	Abduction	Turning the palm down.
b.	Adduction	Moving an arm or leg away from the center of the body.
c.	Extension	Moving a joint in a circle.
d.	Flexion	Moving an arm or leg toward the center of the body.
e.	Pronation	Turning the palm up.
f.	Rotation	Straightening an arm or leg.
g.	Supination	Bending at a joint.

 ACTIVITY 2: PASSIVE RANGE OF MOTION PROCEDURES

Below are some of the steps involved in helping a resident with passive range of motion exercises. Put them in the order you would perform them. Write the number 1 by the first step, etc:

___ Raise the side rail on the far side of the bed.

___ Place the resident in supine position, knees extended, and arms at sides.

___ Document the procedures performed.

___ Perform hand hygiene and explain what you will be doing.

___ Exercise the head and neck, and then move down the body.

___ Provide privacy.

ACTIVITY 3: SHORT ANSWERS

Write short answers in the blanks below:

a. When muscles become weak from disuse it is

   called _____.

b. When a resident performs his own range of motion exercises, it is

   called _____.

c. If muscles and ligaments shorten with disuse, it is

   called _____.

d. Fluid build-up due to inactivity can lead to swelling, edema or

   _____.

e. Pressure sores are also called _____.

ACTIVITY 4: PROBLEMS OF INACTIVITY

Draw a line between each problem in the left column and a possible help or solution in the right column. Some problems may have the same solution:

a. Stasis   Range of motion exercises.

b. Urinary problems   Frequent repositioning.

c. Muscle atrophy   Use of restraints.

d. Constipation   Increasing fluid intake.

e. Pressure sores   Eat more cereals.

Chapter 37: Pressure Ulcers and Positioning

ACTIVITY 1: PRESSURE POINTS

Draw circles at likely places for pressure ulcers. Indicate at least eight:

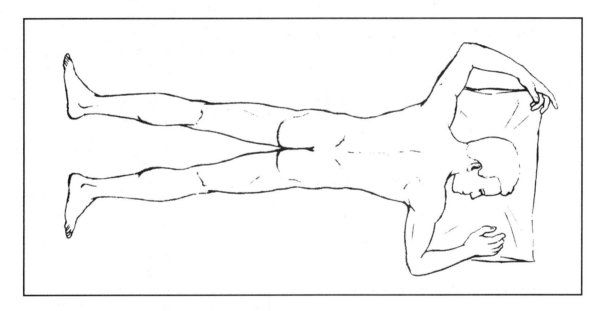

ACTIVITY 2: STAGES OF PRESSURE SORES

Draw a line from the stage in the left column to the appropriate description of that stage in the right column:

a. Stage 1   Breakdown of lower skin tissue.

b. Stage 2   This stage does not exist.

c. Stage 3   Reddened skin.

d. Stage 4   Blistering or breakdown of top layer of skin.

e. Stage 5   Involvement of muscle, nerves and bone.

ACTIVITY 3: PREVENTING PRESSURE ULCERS

Check below five things that are ways to help prevent pressure ulcers:

___ Check shoes and clothing for signs of rubbing.

___ Keep the bedding wrinkle free.

___ Make sure the resident stays in the same position.

___ Apply lotion to the skin to prevent dryness.

___ Use restraints.

___ Protect the skin from scratching or rubbing.

___ Move the patient once every 8 hours.

___ Keep the skin clean and dry.

ACTIVITY 4: PREVENTIVE DEVICE GRID

Find and circle in the grid below eight words or groups of words that refer to activities of daily living:

WORD LIST

EGGCRATE CUSHIONS
WATER MATTRESSES
AIR MATTRESSES
SHEEPSKIN PADS
FOAM RINGS
HEEL PADS
FOOT ELEVATOR
FOOT CRADLE

```
M B F P L Y S Z H A L L R B R C V S
D K O Q O A T E N Y P H O K Z I D Q
S N O W A T E R M A T T R E S S E S
H N T G F G C G U N P N W T A O C X
E B E P B Z F U J B E N Z S X S N W
E M L A L C Y O K I P M G L E D D L
P P E D I C J L O Q H N P Y A A G W
S J V G X B A M S T I Y Z C B E C K
K Q A H I H E R H R C S Z V T L M V
I J T D H W V R M N A R R A J A D G
N D O M F G O A X P V H A M R G P J
P H R N B V O I O I N E J D B D I Z
A J S X R F D X E V A W S J L P B A
D X K T E I T L W C U K H T V E O V
S B V H C A I R M A T T R E S S E S
M N L O G V W H N I Y Z J D T J U C
E G G C R A T E C U S H I O N S O U
O S Q Q Q A H R J A H E E L P A D S
```

ACTIVITY 5: COMPLICATIONS OF INACTIVITY

Check below the likely complications of inactivity:

___ Pain.

___ Meningitis.

___ Arthritis.

___ Pneumonia.

___ Decubitis ulcers.

___ Heart attack.

___ Decreased circulation.

___ Increased temperature.

___ Edema.

___ Contractures.

ACTIVITY 6: POSITIONING

This picture shows a resident in what position? Check the correct answer:

___ Prone

___ Supine

___ Side-lying

___ Semi-supine

___ Ambulating

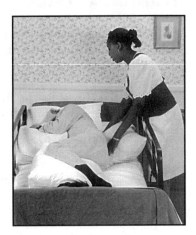

 ACTIVITY 7: PRESSURE ULCERS CROSSWORD

Fill in the crossword below with the pressure ulcer terms that match these definitions:

ACROSS

2. The rear pelvic bone.

4. A tent-like frame at the foot of the bed.

6. Face up.

7. A condition that causes fluid in the lungs.

DOWN

1. Face down.

3. Another term for pressure sores.

5. Swelling due to increased fluid in tissues.

You may use some of the following words:

Ambulation	Coccyx	Edema	Foot belt	Prone
Base	Contracture	Edwina	Iliac	Sheet tent
Brace	Decubitis	Eggcrate	Incline	Stage 1
Center of gravity	ulcers	Foot cradle	Pneumonia	Supine

Chapter 38: Bed Making and Comfort Measures

ACTIVITY 1: MAKING AN UNOCCUPIED BED

Below are some of the steps involved in starting to make an unoccupied bed. Put them in the order you would perform them. Write the number 1 by the first step, etc:

___ Open the sheet at the foot and make sure it is even.

___ Miter the corner.

___ Adjust the bed to a comfortable working height and unfold a bottom sheet lengthwise on it.

___ Tuck the hanging portion of the sheet at the foot of the bed.

___ Remove the soiled linens and place them in a dirty linen container.

___ Raise the mattress to tuck the sheet in at the head.

___ Perform hand hygiene and obtain clean linens.

___ Continue with the bedmaking procedures.

ACTIVITY 2: CHANGING A PILLOWCASE

Below are the steps involved in changing a pillowcase. Put them in the order you would perform them. Write the number 1 by the first step, etc:

___ Bring the pillowcase down over the pillow.

___ Fit the corners of the pillow into the seamless corners of the pillowcase.

___ Fold the extra material from the side seam under the pillow.

___ Place the pillow on the bed with the open end away from the door.

___ Grasp the end of the pillow right through the pillowcase.

___ Hold the pillowcase at the center of the end seam and turn it back over your hand.

ACTIVITY 3: PROVIDING A BACK RUB

Below are some of the steps involved in beginning to provide a back rub. Put them in the order you would perform them. Write the number 1 by the first step, etc:

___ Position the resident with back toward you or face down.

___ Apply the lotion with long firm strokes.

___ Provide privacy.

___ Put lotion on your hands and rub them to warm your hands and lotion.

___ Place the towel lengthwise beside the resident.

___ Assemble the equipment: lotion, basin of water, towel.

___ Place the bottle of lotion in the basin of hot water.

___ Explain what you are going to do and perform hand hygiene.

Activity 4: Providing Perineal Care

Below are some of the steps involved in beginning to provide perineal care. Put them in the order you would perform them. Write the number 1 by the first step, etc:

___ Offer a bedpan or urinal.

___ Provide privacy.

___ Wash perineal area.

___ Assist the resident with the bedpan.

___ Put on gloves.

___ Assemble the equipment; bed protector, bedpan, basin, etc.

___ Place the bed protector under the buttocks.

___ Explain what you will be doing and perform hand hygiene.

Chapter 39: Bathing the Resident

Activity 1: Health Reasons for Bathing

Check below seven reasons that bathing is important:

___ It stimulates circulation.

___ It restores cleanliness by removing dirt and body odors.

___ It provides an opportunity to observe the resident's body for abnormalities.

___ It removes some dangerous bacteria from the skin.

___ It balances the chemical composition of the blood.

___ It provides movement and exercise.

___ It helps the resident relax.

___ It promotes skin integrity.

___ It cures most skin diseases.

Activity 2: Frequent Cleaning

Check any areas listed below that require frequent cleaning:

___ Shins.

___ Hands.

___ Perineal area.

___ Neck.

___ Large smooth areas of skin.

___ Underarms.

___ Face.

___ Bald spots.

___ Creased or folded areas.

___ Chest.

✏ ACTIVITY 3: SAFETY IN BATHING

List below three safety measures that can help in bathing a resident:

_____

_____

_____

✏ ACTIVITY 4: ASSISTING WITH A TUB BATH

Below are some of the steps involved in beginning to assist with a tub bath. Put them in the order you would perform them. Write the number 1 by the first step, etc:

___ Help the resident undress.

___ Fill the tub and test the water for 105 degrees F. Have the resident test it.

___ Provide soap and a washcloth. Help as necessary.

___ Help the resident into the tub.

___ Assemble the equipment on a chair near the tub: towel, soap, washcloth, clean clothing.

___ Place a towel or bath mat on the floor beside the tub.

___ Explain what you are going to do, perform hand hygiene, provide privacy.

✏ ACTIVITY 5: PROVIDING A BED BATH

Below are some of the steps involved in beginning to provide a bed bath, after you have assembled the equipment, plus explained the procedure and provided privacy. Put them in the order you would perform them. Write the number 1 by the first step, etc:

___ Remove the resident's clothing.

___ Cover the resident with a bath blanket.

___ Make the bed flat and raise it to a comfortable working height.

___ Fill the wash basin and provide the bath.

___ Help the resident move closer to you.

___ Offer the resident a bedpan or urinal.

___ Perform hand hygiene and put on gloves.

___ Remove and fold the bedspread and blankets.

Chapter 40: Personal Hygiene

✏️ ACTIVITY 1: ORAL HYGIENE

Check any residents listed below who should be given oral hygiene every two hours:

___ All men.

___ Those who receive oxygen.

___ Those who are feverish.

___ Every resident.

___ Those who are unconscious.

___ Those who breathe through the mouth.

___ Those who ambulate regularly.

___ Those unable to take fluids by mouth.

___ New arrivals.

___ Those with a nasogastric tube.

___ Those who share a room.

___ Those who are vomiting.

✏️ ACTIVITY 2: ORAL HYGIENE

Check below any items that are NOT consequences of poor oral hygiene:

___ Tuberculosis.

___ Bad breath.

___ Dementia.

___ Cavities.

___ Gum disease.

___ High fever.

___ Ear-ringing.

___ Buildup of plaque.

___ Lost teeth.

___ Nasal congestion.

✏️ ACTIVITY 3: CLEANING DENTURES

Below are the steps involved in cleaning dentures, after you have explained the procedure. Put them in the order you would perform them. Write the number 1 by the first step, etc:

___ Place dentures in a clean, rinsed denture cup.

___ Dispose of gloves and perform hand hygiene.

___ Ask the resident for the dentures, or remove them if necessary.

___ Place the dentures in the basin and take it to the sink.

___ Encouraged the resident to rinse his mouth with diluted mouthwash.

___ Brush the dentures with toothpaste and rinse.

___ Replace or store the dentures.

___ Place a towel on the resident's chest and an emesis basin under the chin.

___ Perform hand hygiene and put on gloves.

___ Place paper towels in the sink to prevent breakage.

ACTIVITY 4: SHORT ANSWERS

Fill in the blanks below with appropriate answers:

1. If a resident can take care of his own grooming, he should be

    _____ to do so.

2. While shampooing, the nursing assistant should observe the

    resident's hair and _____.

3. For male residents, shaving should be performed how often?

    _____.

4. Nails should be inspected how often? _____.

5. Dressing a totally dependent resident is easiest if the resident is

    _____.

6. When dressing someone partially paralyzed, you should dress the

    _____ side first.

ACTIVITY 5: ORAL CARE GRID

Find in the grid below words or phrases for five signs you should look for during oral care:

WORD LIST

BLEEDING
SORES
LOOSE TEETH
COATED TONGUE
MOUTH ODOR

```
K I L O O S E T E E T H W R N
W Q K C B W Z Q G B K E U H K
R M G B J U P G H Z G A Z I K
B O C F L I W N U O P E O T M
M U U D U E D I N V U X H N H
M T Q J S V E G E G D D C A E
W H R W Z W Q D N E E F O R O
U O U K A C H O I U M D N F N
R D G V P W T J V N T B Q K A
O O D C Z D Y Q P K G G I V J
R R M A E I T O E N U U T S W
A J S T C U H W X W K R O O Q
Y U A X V T Z P Y T T H V R I
L O Z W Z D P D S J W A K E O
C C E V H Z S E X Z E P W S D
```

ACTIVITY 6: PERSONAL HYGIENE CROSSWORD

Fill in the crossword below with the words that fit the definitions

ACROSS

2. To spit.

3. Care of mouth, teeth, gums.

6. Abrasive stick used in nail care.

7. A film of saliva and germs on teeth.

DOWN

1. Flaking scalp tissue.

4. Feeding device inserted through the nose.

5. Small curved dish that fits under the chin.

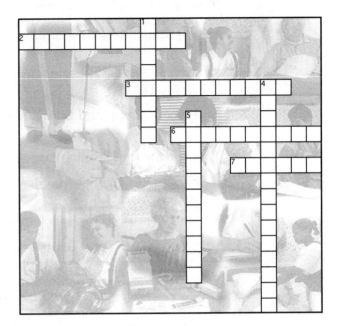

You may use some of the following words:

Ambulant	Dressing	Finger rasp	Personal hygiene
Breathing tube	Edema	Foot belt	Plaque
Cavities	Emery board	Grooming	Spit dish
Contracture	Emesis basin	Nasogastric tube	Tooth paste
Curved dish	Expectorate	Nose insertion	
Decay	Expectant	Oral hygiene	

Chapter 41: Dressings and Bandages

ACTIVITY 1: DRESSINGS, ELASTIC BANDAGES, ELASTIC STOCKINGS

By each use below, indicate which of the three dressings or bandages would most likely be used. Write D for dressing, EB for elastic bandage, or ES for elastic stocking:

___ Hold a dressing in place.

___ Prevent swelling.

___ Protect skin from pressure and rubbing.

___ Protect a wound from germs and dirt.

___ Reduce the development of blood clots.

___ Reduce inflammation of the veins in a leg.

___ Relieve pain.

___ Support the muscle and tissue of a limb.

___ Support the veins of a leg.

ACTIVITY 2: CHANGING A DRESSING

Below are some of the steps involved in beginning to change a dressing, after you have assembled the equipment, plus explained the procedure and provided privacy. Put them in the order you would perform them. Write the number 1 by the first step, etc:

___ Remove the old dressing and dispose of it.

___ Remove gloves and put on new gloves.

___ Tape the dressing in place.

___ Thoroughly cleanse and dry the area.

___ Open the dressing package, but don't touch the dressing.

___ Perform hand hygiene and put on gloves.

___ Cut strips of tape.

___ Apply the new dressing.

ACTIVITY 3: APPLYING AN ELASTIC BANDAGE

Below are the steps involved in applying an elastic bandage, after you have chosen the right size bandage, explained the procedure, washed your hands, and provided privacy. Put them in the order you would perform them. Write the number 1 by the first step, etc:

___ Perform hand hygiene when finished.

___ Wrap the bandage toward the heart with firm, consistent pressure.

___ Document the procedure.

___ Elevate the limb to be wrapped.

___ Ask the resident if the bandage is comfortable.

___ Begin to wrap farthest from the heart.

ACTIVITY 4: SHORT ANSWERS

Write short answers in the blanks below:

a. Elastic stockings should be removed at least every _____.

b. The affected limb should be _____ to help prevent edema.

c. Elastic bandages are applied only if _____.

d. _____ is the most common dressing material.

Chapter 42: IV Care and Tube Feeding

ACTIVITY 1: OBSERVING AN IV

Check below any of the things you may likely be asked to observe about an IV:

___ The color of the fluid.

___ If the drip chamber is full.

___ The rate of flow.

___ If the IV bag is nearly empty.

___ The diameter of the IV tube.

___ The exact height of the IV bottle.

___ If the skin near the IV needle is red.

___ The location of the IV needle.

ACTIVITY 2: SHORT ANSWERS

Write short answers in the blanks below:

a. _____ is used to put fluid directly into a vein.

b. The small area under an IV bag that the fluid drips into is called

   a _____.

c. During tube feeding, the head of the bed should be _____.

d. A machine that is used for tube feeding is called a _____.

Chapter 43: Basic Foods and Fluids

ACTIVITY 1: NUTRIENTS

Check below the items that are types of nutrients:

___ Antibiotics.

___ Carbohydrates.

___ Solids.

___ Platelets.

___ Proteins.

___ Plasma.

___ Vitamins.

___ Food.

___ Air.

___ Fats.

___ Heat.

___ Calories.

ACTIVITY 2: NUTRIENT DEFINITIONS

Draw a line from the word in the left column to the appropriate definition in the right column:

a. Incomplete proteins

b. Carbohydrates

c. Complete proteins

d. Fats

e. Partially complete proteins

f. Vitamins

Proteins that contain all nine amino acids necessary to support life and growth.

Proteins that lack some of the amino acids necessary to support life.

Proteins that are unable to support life or growth.

Substances needed in tiny quantities for specific actions in the body.

The basic energy providers.

Necessary to carry some vitamins and provide energy.

ACTIVITY 3: VITAMINS

Draw a line from the vitamin in the left column to the appropriate function in the body in the right column:

a. Vitamin A

b. Vitamin C

c. Vitamin D

d. Vitamin E

e. Vitamin K

f. B Vitamins

Helps form red blood cells.

Needed for blood clotting and bone metabolism.

Needed for healthy eyes, skin, hair.

Binds cells together and strengthens blood vessels.

Regulates appetite and digestion and many other things.

Helps build teeth and bones.

ACTIVITY 4: FAT-SOLUBLE OR WATER SOLUBLE

For each of the vitamins below indicate whether it is fat soluble or water soluble. Write FS for fat soluble or WS for water soluble:

___ Vitamin A   ___ Vitamin D

___ B Vitamins   ___ Vitamin E

___ Vitamin C   ___ Vitamin K

ACTIVITY 5: MAJOR MINERALS

Draw a line from the mineral in the left column to the appropriate function in the body in the right column:

a. Calcium   Helps regulate fluid balance.

b. Magnesium   Helps build bones and has nerve functions.

                          Builds bones and teeth.

c. Phosphorus

                          Involved in release of energy and bone growth.

d. Potassium

ACTIVITY 6: FOODS WITH MINERALS

Draw a line from the mineral in the left column to the appropriate food source for that mineral in the right column:

a. Calcium   Whole grains and leafy green vegetables.

b. Magnesium   Fruits, nuts, potatoes.

c. Phosphorus   Milk and milk products.

d. Potassium   Meat, poultry and fish.

ACTIVITY 7: TRACE MINERALS GRID

Find in the grid below words or phrases for four trace minerals important in nutrition:

WORD LIST

IRON

IODINE

ZINC

COPPER

```
F T J I M V A H F H
Z I N C N B E I W Y
E P N E U N O W U E
A J Z B I B C Y Y E
Y S S D B O L X M N
K U O F C I R O N Y
M I B D G G B Y S Y
Y U F V H J W H R G
C O P P E R S Y Y A
L A P A P J Y O B N
```

✏ ACTIVITY 8: FOOD PYRAMID

Identify the components of the food pyramid in the spaces below.

Choose from the following:

- Fruits
- Vegetables
- Grains
- Oils

- Meat and Beans
- Physical Activity
- Milk

Chapter 44: Feeding a Resident

 ## ACTIVITY 1: SERVING RESIDENTS IN THE DINING ROOM

Check below the appropriate guidelines for serving residents in the dining room:

___ Protect the resident's clothing with a napkin or bib.

___ Let them choose their own food without checking medical orders.

___ Encourage residents to sit alone.

___ Check to see each resident has all the necessary silverware.

___ Encourage residents to share food from their trays.

___ Perform hand hygiene.

___ If they can feed themselves, no further observation is necessary.

___ Give the resident choices of food on tray when feeding.

___ Assist the resident in cutting up the food, if necessary.

___ Remind residents of the names of other residents sitting nearby.

Activity 2: Serving Residents in Their Rooms

Check below the appropriate guidelines for serving residents in the their rooms:

___ Have the resident sit upright in bed.

___ Put the food tray on his or her lap.

___ Keep the silverware in a separate place from the food tray.

___ Remove the plate covers.

___ Offer as much assistance as needed.

___ Discourage independent eating and assist as much as you can.

___ Verify that it is the correct diet for this resident.

___ Chart what was eaten and how much.

___ Use only plastic knives and forks.

Activity 3: Choking

There are several symptoms of choking. Some indicate a partial obstruction of the airway and others indicate a total obstruction. By each symptom below write PO for partial obstruction and TO for total obstruction:

___ Clutching the throat.

___ Difficulty breathing.

___ High pitched noise caused by a spasm in the larynx.

___ Sudden inability to speak.

___ Sudden inability to cough.

___ Unusual breathing.

___ Wheezing or gurgling in the throat.

Activity 4: The Heimlich Maneuver

Below are the steps involved in performing the Heimlich Maneuver used to clear a blocked airway. Put them in the order you would perform them. Write the number 1 by the first step, etc. NOTE: one of the steps below does NOT belong in the procedure. Cross it out:

___ If it doesn't work, call for assistance and begin CPR.

___ Grasp the fist and make a sharp upward thrust.

___ Perform this six to ten times until the object is expelled.

___ Use your fingers to sweep the mouth to clear any remaining material.

___ Make a fist and place the thumb side in the middle of the abdomen.

___ Stand behind the person and put your arms around his waist.

___ Place the other hand over the fist.

___ Perform hand hygiene first.

Chapter 45: Special Diets

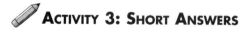 ### ACTIVITY 1: SPECIAL DIETS A

Draw a line from the type of diet in the left column to a type of food in the right column that would likely be eliminated from that diet:

a. Bland

b. Diabetic

c. Full liquid

d. Low fat

e. Low sodium

f. Mechanical soft

Any solid food.

Salty foods.

Spicy foods.

Any large chunks of food.

Sweet ice cream.

Fried foods.

ACTIVITY 2: SPECIAL DIETS B

Draw a line from the condition in the left column to the type of diet in the right column that would likely be prescribed for a person with that condition:

a. Diabetes

b. Overweight

c. Too thin

d. High blood pressure

e. Has missing teeth

f. Following surgery

Low calorie diet.

Mechanical soft diet.

Clear liquid diet.

High calorie diet.

Diabetic diet.

Low sodium diet.

ACTIVITY 3: SHORT ANSWERS

Write short answers in the blanks below:

a. A special diet that eliminates some foods or prepares food in a special way for medical reasons is called a_____.

b. Diets are planned and reviewed by _____.

c. A food that someone is very sensitive to is called _____.

d. A nutritional supplement is often in the form of _____.

ACTIVITY 4: DOCUMENTING INTAKE

Look at the chart of a dinner below, and then answer the questions after it:

MEAL	FOOD	% OF CALORIES
Dinner	Meat, fowl, or fish	40%
	Potato, pasta	20%
	Vegetable	5%
	Bread	10%
	Milk	15%
	Dessert	10%

a. If the resident ate all the food shown, what percentage of the total dinner calories would he have eaten?

_____

b. If the resident ate all the food shown, what percentage of the total dinner calories would have come from starches — potato, pasta, and bread?

_____

c. If the resident ate all the food shown except the meat, fowl, or fish, what percentage of the meat, fowl, or fish calories would he have eaten?

_____

d. If the resident ate all the food shown, what percentage of the total dinner calories would have come from everything EXCEPT desert?

_____

Chapter 46: Elimination Needs

ACTIVITY 1: INCONTINENCE

Check any conditions below that do NOT usually cause incontinence:

___ Tremors or spasms of the bladder.

___ Stress, anxiety or frustration.

___ Arthritis.

___ Central nervous system injury.

___ Urinary tract infection.

___ Lung diseases.

___ Confusion and memory loss.

___ Loss of muscle control.

ACTIVITY 2: GUIDELINES FOR HANDLING INCONTINENCE

Check any actions that are recommended for handling incontinence:

___ Scold the resident who had the accident.

___ Use shame to prevent it happening again.

___ Wear gloves when handling body fluids.

___ Handle it in a calm, professional way.

___ Provide privacy for the resident.

___ Make the resident clean it up himself.

___ Ignore it.

ACTIVITY 3: DANGER POINTS FOR CATHETERS

Draw arrows on the diagram to show where germs can enter the catheter system:

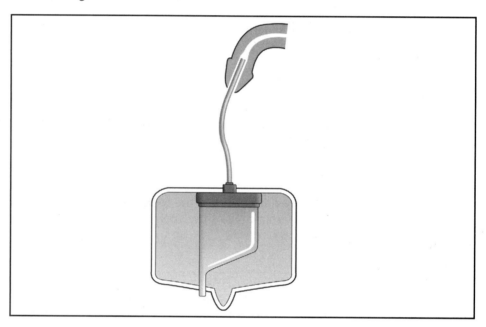

ACTIVITY 4: DAILY CATHETER CARE

Below are some of the steps involved in daily catheter care for a male, after you have assembled equipment, explained the procedure, washed your hands, put on gloves and provided privacy. Put them in the order you would perform them. Write the number 1 by the first step, etc:

___ With a clean wet washcloth, rinse the penis, scrotum and perineal area.

___ Apply soap to a wet washcloth.

___ Make sure the catheter tube is not kinked or pulling.

___ Remove the bed protector and discard it.

___ Clean the four inches of catheter nearest the penis with a new, clean, soapy-wet washcloth.

___ Check the area around the catheter for sores or leakage.

___ Put the bed protector under the resident.

___ Gently pat dry the area.

✏ ACTIVITY 5: SHORT ANSWERS

Fill in the blanks below with appropriate answers

a. If it is necessary to disconnect a catheter drainage tube, you should cover the end of the drainage tube with a _____.

b. A urine collection bag must be positioned _____ the resident's bladder.

c. The opening where urine leaves the body is called the _____.

d. A urine collection bag used for walking is called a _____.

e. The average resident takes in about _____ of liquid every 24 hours.

✏ ACTIVITY 6: INCONTINENCE

Check any symptoms below that usually indicate edema:

___ Swelling of feet.   ___ Swelling of ankle.   ___ Vomiting.

___ Headache.   ___ Increased urinary output.   ___ Decreased urinary output.

___ Joint pain.

___ Weight gain.   ___ Fluid collection in abdomen.

✏ ACTIVITY 7: MEASURING WITH A GRADUATE

Approximately how much liquid is shown in graduate A? _____

Approximately how much liquid is shown in graduate B? _____

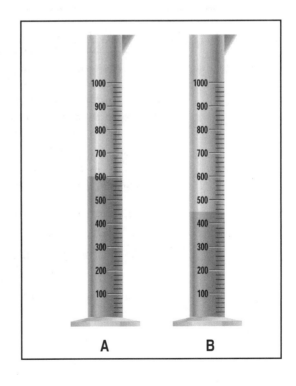

ACTIVITY 8: ELIMINATION CROSSWORD

Fill in the crossword below with the elimination terms that match these definitions:

ACROSS

1. Marked container to measure liquids.
6. A urine collection bag used for walking.

DOWN

1. Moist tissue that lines mouth, nose, eyes.
2. Material that settles out of a liquid.
3. Dryness; fluid output is greater than intake.
4. Excess fluid collecting in tissue.
5. An involuntary muscle contraction.

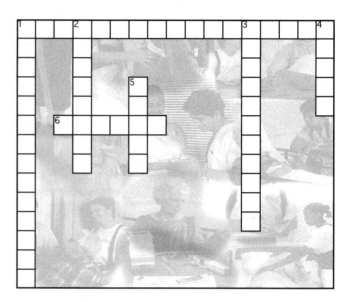

You may use some of the following words:

Amble bag	Emesis	Measuring graduate	Spasm
Breathing tube	Epidermis	Mucous membrane	Spurt
Contracture	Finger rasp	Nasogastric tube	Urinary system
Dehydration	Foot bag	Plaque	
Dressing	Humidity	Sediment	
Edema	Leg bag	Segregate	

Chapter 47: Bladder and Bowel Care

ACTIVITY 1: OFFERING A BEDPAN

Below are some of the steps involved in offering a bedpan, after you have assembled equipment, explained the procedure, washed your hands, put on gloves and provided privacy. Put them in the order you would perform them. Write the number 1 by the first step, etc:

___ Remove the gloves and perform hand hygiene. Return when called.

___ Place a top sheet to provide privacy.

___ Assist the resident in removing or raising lower clothing.

___ Place the bedpan under the resident.

___ Lower the side rail.

___ If the resident can be left unattended, place toilet tissue and a call button in reach.

___ Have the resident bend the knees and raise the hips.

___ Raise the head of the bed if this is allowed.

ACTIVITY 2: USING THE BEDSIDE COMMODE

Below are some of the steps involved in using a bedside commode, after you have assembled equipment, explained the procedure, washed your hands, put on gloves and provided privacy. Put them in the order you would perform them. Write the number 1 by the first step, etc:

___ When the resident calls, respond quickly.

___ Help the resident to the side of the bed, and then have him put on slippers.

___ If the resident can be left unattended, place toilet tissue and a call button in reach.

___ Help transfer the resident to the commode.

___ Dispose of gloves, perform hand hygiene and leave the room.

___ Insert a bedpan under the seat and lock the wheels, if there are wheels.

ACTIVITY 3: URINE COLLECTION

Check the statements that are NOT true of a urine collection.

___ It is a good indication of kidney function.

___ For testing, you need about 75-100 cubic centimeters.

___ Abnormalities are most obvious when the urine is least concentrated.

___ Urine is often tested immediately at bedside.

___ It is best to collect a specimen from the first voiding of the day.

___ It is best to collect a specimen in the evening.

ACTIVITY 4: MIDSTREAM CLEAN-CATCH URINE SPECIMEN

Sometimes a physician order will ask for a urine specimen taken from midstream, not the first flow or last flow. Below are some of the steps involved in collecting a midstream specimen, after you have assembled equipment, explained the procedure, washed your hands, put on gloves and provided privacy. Put them in the order you would perform them. Write the number 1 by the first step, etc:

___ Remove the gloves and perform hand hygiene. Return when called.

___ Pour leftover urine from the bedpan into the toilet.

___ Fill in the label for the container.

___ Offer the bedpan.

___ Thoroughly cleanse the genitals with soap and water or an antiseptic solution.

___ Take the specimen to the charge nurse or to the refrigerator for lab specimens.

___ After the stream has started, place the collection container in the flow and catch the necessary amount.

___ Place the lid and label on the container.

___ Ask the resident to start voiding.

ACTIVITY 5: BOWEL AND BLADDER TRAINING

Check the statements below that are recommended procedures for assisting a resident with bowel and bladder training:

___ Encourage the resident to drink fluids, normally about two quarts daily.

___ Make the resident wait at least one minute after each urge.

___ Make sure the resident eats the prescribed diet.

___ Keep a log of when the resident is incontinent.

___ Keep the resident in bed as much as possible.

___ High fiber foods should be encouraged, if permitted.

___ Respond immediately to a resident's call.

___ Insist that all residents use a bedpan.

ACTIVITY 5: BOWEL AND BLADDER CROSSWORD

Fill in the crossword below with the bowel and bladder terms that match these definitions:

ACROSS

2. Fluid produced by glands.

4. Have a bowel movement.

5. Fluid coughed up from lungs.

DOWN

1. Vomit.

2. Sample of body material for testing.

3. Body system involved in breathing.

4. Body system that digests food.

5. Feces.

You may use some of the following words:

Cardiovascular	Emesis	Respiratory	Sputum
Contracture	Epidermis	Sediment	stool
Defecate	Food tract	Secretion	Urinary system
Detest	Glandular	Spasm	
Digestive Tract	Graduate	Specimen	
Edema	Mucous membrane	Spurt	

Chapter 48: Understanding Behavior

✏ ACTIVITY 1: BASIC NEEDS

List below at least three of Maslow's basic needs:

_____

_____

_____

✏ ACTIVITY 2: MASLOW'S NEEDS

Draw a line from an activity in the left column to one of Maslow's Needs in the right column where that activity would belong. NOTE: there is one need that does not belong. Cross it out:

a. Respect yourself   Basic needs.

b. Food   Security and safety.

c. To dominate others   Love or belonging.

d. Be part of a friendly group

e. Enough money to live   Self-esteem.

f. Feel successful   Self-actualization.

✏ ACTIVITY 3: DEPRESSION

Check the statements below that are NOT true of depression:

___ It can be part of grief.   ___ It usually increases a person's energy.

___ It may cause loss of appetite.

___ It always causes anger.   ___ It can be caused by loss of independence.

___ It may include sleeplessness.

___ It may include too much sleep.   ___ It almost never accompanies loss of loved ones.

ACTIVITY 4: BEHAVIOR

Find and circle in the grid below five words or groups of words that refer to activities of daily living:

WORD LIST

DEPENDENCE
STUBBORNNESS
LOW SELFESTEEM
LOSS
DEPRESSION

```
B W G I Q V G F C Y C V T X G W T L
L O W S E L F E S T E E M M U J R P
U N L F P Y K P T J O W I D O T K I
G V F Z B F R F Q G M Q R A V I G G
R Q D G T U K R L K B I W D D X K M
K M X E M M K A R C B C T K E C B R
Q D Q W P Y B O J G X J V D P J H N
S C O T A E A R Z F U T H W R K D N
H I O Z O K N O S V Y K O H E M W N
T V F B V E G D I N Q M A A S J H D
N C L Z M L A B E A V Q G N S M B B
H Z O I Q W D F H N D S E J I J M K
M W S M S R M M H B C V E U O I U A
O F S P T E M Z L Y A E I T N D M B
L F P T N M W E G N D E W B I D E P
J Z O A Y W L L G B P T L Y L R D Z
D U S S T U B B O R N E S S R W I I
G I Q I L G L N Q N E N N D X L Z Y
```

Chapter 49: Remotivation

ACTIVITY 1: SELF-ESTEEM

Self-esteem can be important to keep a resident motivated. Write below three kinds of compliments you could pay a resident during the day to help:

_____

_____

_____

ACTIVITY 2: SETTING GOALS

Small goals often can lead to larger goals. On the list below some of these actions would generally be small goals, and some generally larger goals. Write SG by the smaller goals and LG by the larger ones:

___ Taking part in activities.

___ A smile.

___ Saying a few words.

___ Signing up for an outside activity.

___ Getting out of bed.

___ Arranging a game with other residents.

___ Remembering the name of another resident.

ACTIVITY 3: NEGATIVE REINFORCEMENT GRID

Find in the grid below words or phrases for five kinds of
reinforcement that you would NOT want to use with the resident:

WORD LIST

SHAME

SCOLDING

ANGER

INSULT

INSINCERITY

```
U W L N J B I E S Q R E W B J
S S A C C Q D D T E Z Y Q S N
H N C H C O Z K C J Y P U F T
I H K O E O S H A M E V K Q D
V D V S L S L M N X S M S Y P
F O W Z S D Y N G C H F T V C
G N V H Y J I K D L X I Q F S
S L Y C T Y R N I L R U D K R
Y T W J E T Z G G E Z F N G S
Z A N G E R P G C G D V Y V H
B W H S I N C N P B D U K T G
F A M V I O I Q W A P O A J P
E Z N U Q S I F I I N S U L T
I I T U N S J Z U W Y S J I G
C M B I B Q C S F W V D F I N
```

Chapter 50: Psychosocial Needs

 ACTIVITY 1: PSYCHOSOCIAL NEEDS

Check the items below that do NOT represent positive psychosocial needs:

___ To be appreciated.   ___ To be recognized.

___ To have shelter.   ___ To have plenty of food.

___ To feel worthwhile.   ___ To be respected.

___ Depression.   ___ To have enemies.

___ A sense of accomplishment.

 ACTIVITY 2: SUGGESTED RESPONSES

Below are a series of things you might say to a resident. Check the
ones that are NOT appropriate and helpful:

___ "You shouldn't feel that way."   ___ "Everybody here dislikes you
                                              when you do that."
___ "I'll help you get to know your
    neighbors."   ___ "Would you like to try to walk?"

___ "I understand how you feel,   ___ "What would you like to wear
    sweetie."   today?"

___ "I'll be right there to help you."   ___ "Comb your hair. You look
                                              terrible."
___ "Where did you used to live?"

___ "Get over it. Everybody has to."

Chapter 51: Socialization Needs

✎ ACTIVITY 1: SOCIALIZATION

Check below the positive things that socialization generally provides:

___ Food.   ___ Clothing.

___ Affection.   ___ Stimulation.

___ Ideas.   ___ Information.

___ Anger.   ___ Opportunity to show anger.

___ Support.   ___ Opportunity to show affection.

✎ ACTIVITY 2: ROLE CHANGE

When a person becomes a resident, often some roles in life are lost. Write below three possible role losses that a man might face:

_____

_____

_____

✎ ACTIVITY 3: HELPING SOCIALIZATION

In the list below, check any of the following that are recommended ways to help a resident's socialization:

___ Introduce residents to others.

___ Make sure they can't leave social activities.

___ Try to get roommates to become friends.

___ Discourage writing to those outside the facility.

___ Preserve as much of the previous lifestyle as possible.

___ Be friendly with family who visit.

___ Help the resident call or write friends.

___ Remind the resident of all the people who have not come to visit.

Chapter 52: Intervention and Substance Abuse

ACTIVITY 1: INTERVENTIONS

Draw a line from a problem activity in the left column to a possible intervention for that problem in the right column. NOTE: there is one intervention that does not belong. Cross it out:

a. Apathy

A calm friendly approach.

b. Anxiety

Find other ways for the resident to gain some control over his life.

c. Manipulation

Listen but be firm in insisting the resident get up, get dressed, and eat.

d. Depression

Active friendliness and praise.

Get angry and insist you are the boss.

e. Uncooperativeness

Let the resident know you care and want to help.

f. Combativeness

Make it clear what you will and will not do.

g. Confusion

Stay calm and move away.

ACTIVITY 2: NECESSARY DEMANDS

Check below demands that you MUST insist the resident follow:

___ Wear appropriate clothing.

___ He cannot harm others.

___ She must eat her full meal.

___ He cannot leave the facility.

___ She must use the bathroom regularly.

___ He cannot use televisions.

___ She must take her medications.

ACTIVITY 3: SUBSTANCE ABUSE

Check below any signs that might indicate substance abuse and should be watched:

___ Forgetfulness.

___ Friendliness.

___ Rapid speech or behavior.

___ Taking part in activities.

___ Mood swings.

___ Angry outbursts.

___ Visits from family.

___ Unexplained drowsiness.

___ Incontinence.

___ Sudden changes in behavior.

Chapter 53: Role Changes

✏ ACTIVITY 1: LIFE ROLE GRID

Find in the grid below words or phrases for six factors that help determine a person's role in life:

WORD LIST

GENDER

AGE

RELATIONSHIP

OCCUPATION

SPECIAL INTERESTS

ILLNESS

```
O C C U P A T I O N Z Y L I S F X I
P N I I C S I S D C C F J E B E E L
X W S W I Q V H W V A A I Z B P E L
W T A U G L R E W O T Y G K D M C N
I Y I G S R W E G P F F C E G Y E E
C W N C K F C J L P T Y B Z B U Z S
U O W R M O V V D A H Y E P Q M D S
G E N D E R U P Q X T A R B C J W N
L L E A N K F K Z D J I D D C T J X
P B H P C K F C X D H S O G Q P M W
A V U F J D K Z P M W N H N P V B C
P C S S U I G O V K G E D Y S Z D Z
U A P X S A P J N A R E G F Q H O L
S P E C I A L I N T E R E S T S I Z
U Z Z R W X I I C O X E Q M V J S P
Q V W T D U O J S K F Y N P H S C L
W S R V C A F B N J T Q A V C R R S
Q H O Y I U V S L N S I G M Z Z D V
```

✏ ACTIVITY 2: ROLES

At the moment you are a student. This is a role. Write below at least three other roles in life that you presently fulfill:

Student _____

_____

_____

_____

Chapter 54: Dementia and Confusion

ACTIVITY 1: DEGREES OF DEMENTIA

For each of the symptoms below, indicate whether it would be most characteristic of mild, moderate or severe dementia. Write MI for mild, MO for moderate, SE for severe:

___ Bed-ridden.

___ Having a sudden tantrum.

___ Forgets recent events.

___ Loss of fairly old memories.

___ Can't speak.

___ Carelessness.

___ Loss of attention span.

___ Not focused.

___ Grows worse in early evening.

___ Wandering.

___ Disorientation.

___ Repeating words.

___ Seizures.

ACTIVITY 2: DEALING WITH ARGUING AND AGGRESSION

Check below the actions that are NOT recommended for dealing with arguing and aggression:

___ Argue back until you convince them.

___ Offer diversions.

___ Get angry.

___ Stay calm.

___ Always explain what you are doing.

___ Mock the person.

___ Keep to a simple routine.

ACTIVITY 3: DEALING WITH WANDERING

Check below the actions that are recommended for dealing with wandering:

___ Keep familiar objects nearby.

___ Lock the person in his or her room.

___ Keep outside doors closed or alarmed.

___ Keep the person on a 20 foot leash.

___ Cover a doorknob, if feasible.

___ Keep the person heavily sedated.

ACTIVITY 4: REALITY ORIENTATION

Check below all the actions that ARE recommended to help keep a person with mild dementia oriented:

___ Use your own name and their name often.

___ Speak clearly and simply.

___ Tattoo their name to their arm.

___ Keep to a routine.

___ Don't ask questions that require memory.

___ Give them surprises.

___ Work the date and location into your talk.

___ Treat them with dignity, as adults.

ACTIVITY 5: DEMENTIA WORD GRID

Find and circle in the grid below eight words that refer to dementia:

WORD LIST

DEPRESSION

CLINGING

HOARDING

NONRECOGNITION

UNDRESSING

STEALING

SUNDOWNING

WANDERING

```
M X D U B U V L V X B E X H C T C D X W
A N I W N M B O H S Y N H Z I O W E Z T
N O H L Q D X H S V E J Z H K P G P E S
K N N W A I R O Z H O A R D I N G R X U
M R C F T C I E I Y M V C E U O Q E W I
F E K B G E Q Y S F P W Q J H R C S M B
H C R R A X J A S S N R O H T L B S C T
U O T K L M G T C T I A K I D F P I Z G
I G A U E O X C Q F A N E U G H I O E I
L N A H T E A U C H E T G B O P D N J I
K I Y B Y R S R Y L Z P H W Z K G J V S
D T F K Y F V Q F J I N E B J J Z T Y U
H I D V V J U G M P B N J G L X F O B N
M O L O W T N P F Y E G G Q U L Y C K D
H N Y U Q I V D O M V P J I V T D E O O
M T B Y L N G W M X A X I B N V U P J W
D Z D A L R A S P R P A J O T G Q T T N
D A E K U C R B Q D U J J V U X Z L G I
C T W F U T P W A N D E R I N G W A I N
S I E L R D G S Z V M J X X I P F O R G
```

Chapter 55: Sexuality

✏️ ## ACTIVITY 1: MYTHS ABOUT SEXUALITY

Below are seven statements about sexuality and the elderly. For each, write M for myth or F for fact:

___ The physical exercise of sex is good for older people.

___ Sex is only for procreation.

___ Sexual attraction is much more than looking young and beautiful.

___ Old people are not interested in sex.

___ Sex is too strenuous for old people.

___ Many older people continue to enjoy sexual activity into old age.

___ Old people should act their age and give up sex.

✏️ ## ACTIVITY 2: SEXUAL CHANGES WITH AGE

List below one physical change with aging that affects sexuality for men and women:

Men: _____

Women: _____

✏️ ## ACTIVITY 3: SEXUALITY AND THE ELDERLY

Check below activities that are recommended in dealing with a resident's sexuality:

___ Respect the privacy of their rooms.

___ Discourage all sexual expression.

___ Help the residents feel attractive.

___ Treat all the residents as sexually neutral.

___ Don't expose their private parts unnecessarily.

___ Listen to their sexual concerns.

___ Make them feel guilty about sexual desires.

Chapter 56: Culture and Religion

✏️ ACTIVITY 1: HELPING WITH SPIRITUAL NEEDS

Check below activities that are recommended for helping a resident with spiritual needs:

___ Providing privacy for religious observances.

___ Arguing which is the best religion.

___ Trying to learn about their religion.

___ Helping residents respect one another's religions.

___ Refuse to talk about religion at all.

___ Helping residents attend services.

___ Take religious articles away from residents.

___ Notify the charge nurse if a resident wants a clergy visit.

___ Treat religious articles with respect.

✏️ ACTIVITY 2: RELIGION AND FOODS

With which religion would you associate the following food or food custom? Write the religion in the blank:

a. A fast called Ramadan. _____

b. Eating fish on Friday. _____

c. Eating only kosher food. _____

d. Eating pork but not taking alcohol. _____

e. Vegetarian. _____

f. Eating only halal foods. _____

g. Eating special foods during Passover. _____

h. Giving up a certain food for Lent. _____

ACTIVITY 3: CULTURE AND RELIGION CROSSWORD

Fill in the crossword below with the words that fit the definitions:

ACROSS

1. Roman Catholic prayer beads.

3. The Moslem holy book.

6. A Christian fast before Easter.

7. Acceptable in Jewish dietary laws.

8. A Jewish holiday in the spring.

DOWN

2. Jewish skull cap.

4. Acceptable for a Moslem to eat.

5. A Jewish holiday, in the winter.

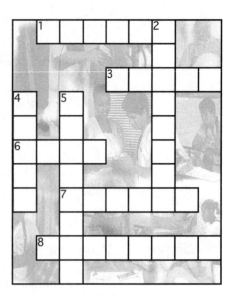

You may use some of the following words:

Bible	Fish	Kosher	Saint
Bishop	Gospel	Lent	Sentiment
Christmas	Halal	Mardi Gras	Star
Cross	Hanukkah	Mormon	Worry beads
Digestive	Haganah	Passover	Yarmulke
Easter	Kepi	Ramadan	
Edible	Koran	Rosary	

Chapter 57: Death and Dying

 ACTIVITY 1: STAGES OF DYING

Dr. Kubler-Ross identified five stages that many people go through when they are faced with dying. The stages are listed below, plus one that does not belong. Cross out the one that does not belong and put the rest in order. Write 1 by the first stage, etc:

___ Acceptance.   ___ Bargaining.

___ Anger.   ___ Denial.

___ Apathy.   ___ Depression.

ACTIVITY 2: ASSISTING THE DYING

Check below activities that are NOT recommended for assisting the dying:

___ Avoid all laughter and cheerfulness.

___ Swab the mouth with glycerine if it is dry.

___ Darken the room.

___ Respect the resident's view of death and the afterlife even if it isn't your own.

___ Report any requests for clergy.

___ Speak in a whisper.

___ Listen if the resident wants to talk.

___ Assume the resident can hear everything said in the room.

___ Be friendly, accepting and natural.

ACTIVITY 3: POSTMORTEM CARE

Below are some of the steps involved in beginning to provide postmortem care. Put them in the order you would perform them. Write the number 1 by the first step, etc:

___ Bathe the body and replace any soiled dressings.

___ Perform hand hygiene and put on gloves.

___ Close the eyes. If necessary use a damp cotton ball.

___ Assemble the necessary equipment.

___ Identify the resident and provide privacy.

___ Place the body on the back, with a pillow under head and shoulders.

___ Replace dentures in the mouth if they are out.

Chapter 58: Using A Computer

✏ ACTIVITY 1: PARTS OF A COMPUTER

Fill in the blank next to each part using the words in the list below.

- CPU

- USB flash drive

- keyboard

- monitor

- mouse

- CD/DVD

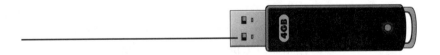

ACTIVITY 2: SOFTWARE

Put the letter of the function on the right beside the appropriate kind of software on the left.

___ Communications Program.

___ Data Management.

___ Desktop Publisher.

___ Graphics Program.

___ Spreadsheet.

___ Web Browser.

___ Word Processor.

a. Makes newsletters and leaflets.

b. Finds information on the Internet.

c. Sends and receives e-mail.

d. Keeps accounts and manages finances.

e. Stores and files data.

f. Types documents.

g. Draws pictures.

ACTIVITY 3: COMPUTERS CROSSWORD

Fill in the crossword below with the words that fit the definitions:

ACROSS

1. A small, removable memory device that fits into a USB port and can hold a large amount of data.

5. Software to find information on the Internet.

6. The screen where you can read what is entered into the computer.

7. The device where you can press buttons to enter data.

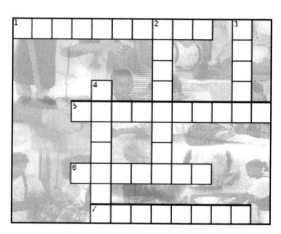

DOWN

2. The network of computers all over the world.

3. A device that moves the cursor when you move it on the desktop.

4. A group of linked computers, usually in one location.

You may use some of the following words:

Monitor	Scanner	Network	Internet
CD-ROM	Cursor	E-mail	Word Processor
Mouse	Server	Spreadsheet	Keyboard
CPU	Flash Drive	Icon	Web Browser

Chapter 59: Your Career in Healthcare

✎ ACTIVITY 1: LOOKING FOR JOB OPENINGS

Look over the list of people and places below. Write Y (for YES) beside any that would be a likely place to consult for a CNA job opening. Write N (for NO) beside any that you do NOT think are very likely places to find out about job openings

___ Friend who works in a hospital.

___ Friend who works in a drug store.

___ Classified ads in the newspaper.

___ Employment agencies.

___ Newspaper front page.

___ Machine shop.

___ A local nursing home.

___ A website for a hospital.

___ A CNA teacher.

___ A high school physics teacher.

___ A supermarket bulletin board.

___ A school's placement service.

✎ ACTIVITY 2: JOB INTERVIEW

Look over the list of questions below. Write Y (for YES) beside any that you would likely be asked in a job interview. Write N (for NO) beside any that you do NOT think you are very likely to be asked.

___ What is your favorite color?

___ What made you want to become a CNA?

___ Do you have any relatives in healthcare?

___ Would you be willing to work for half the minimum wage?

___ Have you had trouble with a supervisor on any earlier job?

___ Could we count on you to work an 80-hour week?

___ Why do you want a job at our facility?

___ What do you think you won't like about this facility?

___ Who did you vote for for president?

___ Can you start today?

ACTIVITY 3: CAREER PATH GRID

In the following letter grid, find and circle six words or phrases that describe healthcare careers:

WORD LIST

PHLEBOTOMY

SPEECH THERAPY

RADIOLOGY

FOOD SERVICES

PHYSICAL THERAPY

REGISTERED NURSING

```
X C R R S L V A Y J P P F F V D G S A C W W F N
K G E N K H L M U S F X I S H N V U H U F V G W
B J X G Q G W U W I W J N O I B Y N F A P G M Z
T Y T L C O N L W J J D C M Y H K M D S H Z E B
K B Q A P W G W K B H E P M B I J X S G G H G N
N K L W O U I U B R H G O L B V I R P T H Y C T
H R F O K X P F R M Z T L Z B S F E C H C E R J
L Q E F Y N Q H F S O C H T E Q Q G Z G C W I S
F Z G V X O L U Y B X Q Y F C G V I U O C B S S
O R W I G V C E E S G E S N W S H S M C N A P Z
O J J M C S G L G X I L T I C O W T N N L D E Y
D B I G N Y H H E I Y C V B H G B E D Z I B E E
S A A G Z P R V V J Y Y A P G Y R R P H K O C J
E E F D Z V A X L M V Z L L C X W E M V F U H G
R T O Z Z R X X B R A G X N T N V D T Z Z W T Z
V Y Z T G A W G O A T Q G E F H W N L N J V H Y
I I G H S D M Q P Z Y F N I S I E U J C G B E C
C G V O W I W J J U B G B L J Z E R T U W S R M
E L G E R O S F F T V F F R W E U S A L Y P A J
S A Y G Z L T X P R H U T E M H M I L P C R P M
C Z P R N O B J S U B B T X J N C N C Q Y I Y C
P P S C Y G Y F V Q T K C Y J C Y G F W T H A I
V U U P Y Y Q U Y C U E G P Z A R R I Z Q V W N
E G K O L D V E J Y M I H A Y F T T O V Z K K H
```

THE NEW NURSING ASSISTANT SKILLS CHECKLISTS

SKILLS CHECKLISTS

The New Nursing Assistant
Skills Checklists

Chapter 8 Skills Checklists:
Admissions: Assisting with a Baseline Assessment

Name: _____   Date: _____

Procedures	Y	N	Comments
1. Perform hand hygiene.			
2. Assembles equipment needed in resident unit:			
• admission checklist, worksheet, or chart			
• thermometer			
• stethoscope			
• blood pressure gauge			
• watch with second hand			
• scale			
• urine specimen cup and rubber gloves (if required)			
• gown or pajamas (if used in facility)			
3. Identifies resident.			
4. Double checks resident's name against paperwork.			
5. Explains procedure to resident.			
6. Asks family and friends to wait in lobby or waiting area.			
7 Provides privacy for resident.			
8. Assists nurse as required.			

Checked by: _____

Date signed off *(meets all criteria)*: _____

The New Nursing Assistant
Skills Checklists

Chapter 10 Skills Checklists:
Admissions: Transfers, Discharges and Homecare

Name: _____ Date: _____

Procedures	Y	N	Comments
PREPARING FOR A TRANSFER			
1. Makes sure resident or family has given permission for transfer.			
2. Makes sure resident knows reasons for transfer.			
3. Explains when and how transfer will happen.			
4. Shares helpful care information about resident with nurse and nursing assistant in new area.			
5. If possible, has nurse or nursing assistant from new area come over and meet resident before transfer.			
ASSISTING WITH THE TRANSFER			
1. Makes sure new room is prepared before beginning.			
2. Obtains wheelchair, bed or cart to be used for transfer.			
3. Obtains any portable medical equipment that must move with patient, ex., IV stand.			
4. Perform hand hygiene.			
5. Checks resident's identification bracelet.			
6. Makes very sure right resident being moved.			
7. Explains procedure to resident.			
8. Collects resident's valuables from unit and lists them, if necessary.			
9. Either has resident place all valuables in clearly marked bag or envelope, or does it with resident watching.			
10. Provides privacy for resident.			
11. Helps resident into robe and slippers if allowed.			
12. Collects any medication, plus chart and nursing plan to transfer with resident.			
13. Assists nurse or transfer team with transfer.			
14. Remains cheerful and reassures resident.			

Procedures	Y	N	Comments
ASSISTING WITH THE ARRIVAL			
1. Helps resident into bed or into chair, if he or she is allowed to sit up.			
2. Makes sure any roommates and local nursing staff are introduced to resident.			
3. Transfers valuables, chart, and medications to local nursing staff.			
4. Helps put these away if necessary.			
5. Helps explain to resident anything that is different from old room, and any different procedures.			
6. Answers any questions resident may have, or makes sure there is someone there who can answer them.			
7. Makes sure resident feels as comfortable as possible.			
8. Perform hand hygiene.			
9. Completes any documentation necessary to describe transfer.			
DISCHARGES			
1. Makes sure physician has approved discharge.			
2. Obtains wheelchair or other vehicle.			
3. Perform hand hygiene.			
4. Helps resident dress, if possible.			
5. Explains what is happening.			
6. Helps resident gather his or her belongings, if necessary.			
7. Checks in all drawers and closets.			
8. Helps family or resident gather any valuables placed in safe keeping in facility.			
9. Checks with nurse for any medications or medical equipment that must go with resident.			

Procedures	Y	N	Comments
10. When appropriate vehicle arrives, assists in moving resident to discharge exit of facility and into vehicle.			
11. Bids resident and any family farewell.			
12. Returns to unit, strips bed, and prepares it for another resident.			
13. Perform hand hygiene.			

Checked by: _____

Date signed off *(meets all criteria)*: _____

Chapter 20 Skills Checklists:
Infection Control

Name: _____   Date: _____

Procedures	Y	N	Comments
Performing hand hygiene with an antiseptic hand rub.			
1. Apply the manufacturer's recommended amount of the agent to the palm of one hand.			
2. Rub the hands together so the agent covers all surfaces of the hands and fingers.			
3. Continue to rub until the hands are dry. Do not rinse			
PERFORM HAND HYGIENE			
1. Keeping fingertips down, completely wets own hands and wrists under warm running water.			
2. Applies soap and spreads over both hands and wrists, including between fingers, and under nails. (Uses antimicrobial agent if there was contact with infective material, such as fecal material or wound drainage.)			
3. For one full minute, vigorously rubs hands together:			
• between fingers			
• under nails			
• two inches above wrists			
4. Rinses under warm running water, holding fingers down.			
5. Dries hands thoroughly with paper towels.			
6. Dries wrists thoroughly with paper towels.			
7. Turns off faucet with paper towel between faucet and own hand.			
8. Immediately discards towel. Faucets are considered dirty and will contaminate hands.			

Procedures	Y	N	Comments
LINEN HANDLING			
1. Perform hand hygiene before touching clean linen.			
2. Holds clean linen away from own body to prevent transfer of microorganisms to clean linen from uniform.			
3. Holds soiled linen away from own body to prevent transfer of microorganisms to uniform.			
4. Avoids shaking or fluffing linen, as this spreads microorganisms.			
5. Never places soiled linen on bedside furniture or floor.			
6. Soiled linen must be placed immediately in soiled linen hamper and lid must be tightly closed.			
7. Perform hand hygiene immediately after handling soiled linen.			

Checked by: _____

Date signed off *(meets all criteria)*:_____

Chapter 25 Skills Checklists:
Measuring Weight and Height

Name: _____   Date: _____

Procedures	Y	N	Comments
MEASURING WEIGHT			
1. Weighs resident at same time each day to eliminate effect of weight fluctuates during day. (Best time to weigh resident is first thing in morning, before resident has anything to eat or drink.)			
2. Has resident empty his or her bladder before measuring weight.			
3. Weighs resident on same scale every time to avoid inconsistencies between different scales.			
4. Has resident wear same clothing each time he or she is weighed to avoid differences in clothing weight.			
5. Has resident wear as little clothing as possible while maintaining resident's privacy.			
6. Records weight.			
7. Notes anything that artificially increases resident's weight, such as presence of brace, prosthesis, or cast.			
8. If possible, takes resident to scales and avoids moving scales, since moving may cause inaccurate measurements.			
9. Always checks scale for proper balance by pushing weights to zero with no one on it and checking that scale balances.			
The Standing Balance Scale			
1. If resident being admitted, asks resident what his or her normal weight is.			
2. If scheduled weighing of previously admitted resident, notes previous weight from resident's chart.			
3. Explains procedure to resident.			

Procedures	Y	N	Comments
4. Perform hand hygiene.			
5. Puts gait belt on resident for support.			
6. Takes resident to scale.			
7. Checks scale for proper balance prior to having resident stand on it.			
8. Assists resident onto scale.			
9. Makes sure resident stands on center of scale with arms at sides.			
10. Holds onto resident's gait belt for support and to prevent resident from losing balance.			
11. Lets go only for a moment while measurement actually taken.			
12. Remains prepared to immediately hold belt again if resident needs support.			
13. Adjusts weights until scale is balanced.			
14. Reads weight and writes down immediately.			
15. Places weights back to zero.			
16. Assists resident off scale.			
17. Assists resident back to room.			
18. Removes gait belt from resident's waist.			
19. Perform hand hygiene.			
20. Notifies charge nurse if there is increase or decrease in resident's weight from last weighing.			
21. Records weight in resident's medical chart.			
Wheelchair Scale			
1. If resident being admitted, asks resident what his or her normal weight is. If resident being re-weighed, checks resident's chart and notes previous weight.			
2. Explains procedure to resident.			
3. Perform hand hygiene.			
4. Takes resident's wheelchair to scale.			

Procedures	Y	N	Comments
5. Checks scale for balance prior to putting resident on scale.			
6. Pushes empty wheelchair onto scale.			
7. Adjusts weights until scale is balanced			
8. Reads weight, and writes down immediately.			
9. Places resident into same wheelchair, reverses wheelchair, and pushes it onto scale so resident is facing away from scale.			
10. Locks wheelchair brakes.			
11. Adjusts weights until scale is balanced.			
12. Reads weight and writes down immediately			
13. Puts weights back to zero.			
14. Unlocks brakes.			
15. Rolls wheelchair off scale.			
16. Subtracts weight of empty wheelchair from weight of resident in wheelchair. Result is resident's weight.			
17. Perform hand hygiene.			
18. Notifies charge nurse if weight loss or gain from last weighing.			
19. Records resident's weight in chart.			
Mechanical Lift Scale			
1. Moves mechanical lift scale next to resident's bed.			
2. Explains procedure to resident.			
3. Provides privacy for resident.			
4. Perform hand hygiene.			
5. If resident being admitted, asks resident what his or her normal weight is.			
6. If resident being re-weighed, checks resident's chart and notes previous weight.			

Procedures	Y	N	Comments
7. Has resident lie flat on his or her back.			
• Rolls resident onto one side.			
• Places half of sling between resident's shoulders and knees.			
• Rolls resident to opposite side, and pulls other half of sling under resident.			
8. Places lift scale over resident with base under bed			
9. Attaches sling to scale using hooks provided. (Open part of hook should be away from resident.)			
10. Uses hand crank or pump handle to raise resident.			
• Buttocks should be clear of bed.			
• Resident should be aligned comfortably in sling.			
• If resident's body is not touching bed, weight can be taken at this point.			
• If body is touching bed, proceeds with steps 11 and 12.			
11. Swings resident's feet and legs over edge of bed.			
12. Moves lift away from bed so that resident's body not touching bed.			
13. Adjusts weights until scale is balanced.			
14. Reads weight and writes down immediately.			
15. Moves resident back over bed.			
16. Slowly releases knob which lowers resident onto bed.			
17. Unhooks sling and gently removes it from under resident.			
18. Returns mechanical lift scale to its proper storage area.			
19. Perform hand hygiene.			
20. Notifies charge nurse if weight loss or gain from last weighing.			
21. Records weight in resident's chart.			

Chapter 25 Skills Checklists: Measuring Weight and Height

Procedures	Y	N	Comments
MEASURING HEIGHT			
Measuring Residents Who Can Stand			
1. Explains procedure to resident.			
2. Perform hand hygiene.			
3. Has resident stand facing away from scale.			
4. Raises measuring rod above resident's head.			
5. Lowers rod until it rests gently on top of resident's head.			
6. Reads measurement.			
7. Assists resident off scale.			
8. Returns resident to room.			
9. Records measurement in resident's chart.			
10. Perform hand hygiene.			
Measuring Stooped Residents			
1. Explains procedure to resident.			
2. Perform hand hygiene.			
3. Has resident stand up, assisting as needed.			
4. Measures resident from top of head to shoulder using tape measure.			
• Writes this measurement down.			
5. Measures from shoulder to heel.			
• Writes measurement down.			
6. Calculates resident's height by adding two measurements together.			
7. Records height measurement in resident's medical chart.			
8. Perform hand hygiene.			

MEDCOM TRAINEX® © 2003, 2004, 2010, Medcom Inc. All rights reserved. Page 115

Procedures	Y	N	Comments
Measuring Residents in Bed			
1. Explains procedure to resident.			
2. Provides privacy for resident.			
3. Perform hand hygiene.			
4. Positions resident so he or she is lying flat and straight on bed.			
5. Marks sheet at top of resident's head and at bottom of resident's heels using pen or pencil.			
6. Rolls resident on to one side.			
7. Measures distance between two marks on sheet using tape measure, and writes down.			
8. Rolls resident back.			
9. Records measurement in resident's medical chart.			
10. Perform hand hygiene.			
Measuring Residents With Contractures			
1. Explains procedure to resident.			
2. Provides privacy for resident.			
3. Perform hand hygiene			
4. Positions resident on his or her back in bed.			
5. Using a tape measure, measures from top of heads to bottom of buttocks.			
• Writes this measurement down.			
6. Measures from top of legs to knee.			
• Writes down this measurement.			
7. Measures from knees to heel.			
• Writes down this measurement.			
8. Adds these three measurements together. Sum is resident's height.			
9. Records this height measurement in resident's medical chart.			
10. Perform hand hygiene.			

Checked by: _____

Date signed off *(meets all criteria)*:_____

Chapter 26 Skills Checklists:
Measuring Vital Signs

Name: _____   Date: _____

Procedures	Y	N	Comments
TAKING TEMPERATURES			
Oral Temperature			
1. Assembles necessary equipment:			
• oral thermometer			
• paper towel			
• disposable sleeve			
• pen			
• paper			
2. Perform hand hygiene.			
3. Explains procedure to resident.			
4. Puts on disposable gloves.			
5. Provides privacy for resident.			
6. If thermometer has been soaking in disinfectant, rinses it with cool water			
7. Dries thermometer with paper towel.			
8. Inspects thermometer.			
9. Never uses chipped or cracked thermometer.			
10. Shakes mercury down by holding thermometer between thumb and forefinger and shaking it with snapping motion of wrist, away from furniture or equipment.			
11. Holding end of thermometer away from bulb, inserts bulb end into disposable sleeve.			
12. Removes any pull-off covering from sleeve.			
13. Does not touch end of thermometer that goes into resident's mouth.			
14. Places bulb end of thermometer under resident's tongue.			
15. Asks resident to keep his or her mouth closed.			

Procedures	Y	N	Comments
16. Leaves it in place for at least three minutes. Temperature is more accurate if left in place for five minutes.			
17. Never leaves resident with a thermometer in place.			
18. Removes thermometer from resident's mouth.			
19. Observes tip of column of mercury. It will be easier to read if held at eye level with one's back to a light source.			
20. Removes and discards gloves.			
21. Discards sleeve.			
22. Immediately writes down temperature readings.			
23. Transfers this information to resident's medical chart.			
24. Perform hand hygiene.			
25. Reports any abnormal temperature readings to charge nurse.			
Using A Digital Thermometer			
1. Using a digital thermometer is the same except for the following differences:			
• Covers probe with disposable sleeve.			
• Leaves in place until it beeps or buzzes.			
• Simply reads digital display and makes note of it.			
• Discards disposable sleeve.			
Rectal Temperature			
1. Assembles necessary equipment:			
• rectal thermometer			
• paper towel			
• gloves			
• lubricating jelly			
• pen			
• paper			

Procedures	Y	N	Comments
2. Perform hand hygiene.			
3. Explains procedure to resident.			
4. Provides for privacy.			
5. Inspects thermometer.			
6. Never uses a chipped or cracked thermometer.			
7. If necessary, shakes thermometer down.			
8. Puts sleeve over thermometer.			
9. Places small amount of lubricating jelly on paper towel.			
10. Uses it to lubricate bulb end of rectal thermometer. This will make insertion easier and more comfortable. (There may be lubrication inside sleeve also.)			
11. Puts on protective gloves.			
12. Turns resident to side.			
13. Lifts resident's upper buttock until anus is exposed.			
14. Gently inserts bulb end of thermometer about one inch into rectum.			
15. Holds in place three minutes.			
16. Never leaves resident with thermometer in place.			
17. Removes thermometer.			
18. Discards thermometer sleeve.			
19. Reads temperature.			
20. Removes gloves.			
21. Discards gloves.			
22. Writes temperature down on paper immediately.			
• Uses letter "R" after temperature to indicate it was taken rectally.			
23. Records it in resident's medical chart.			
24. Perform hand hygiene.			
25. Reports any abnormal reading to charge nurse immediately.			

MEDCOM TRAINEX®
Page 119

Procedures	Y	N	Comments
Axillary Temperature			
1. Assembles necessary equipment:			
• oral thermometer			
• paper towel			
• pen			
• paper			
2. Perform hand hygiene.			
3. Explains procedure to resident.			
4. Provides privacy for resident.			
5. If thermometer has been soaking in disinfectant, rinses it with cool water.			
6. Dries thermometer with paper towel.			
7. Inspects thermometer.			
8. Never uses chipped or cracked thermometer.			
9. Shakes mercury down on thermometer.			
10. Puts disposable sleeve on thermometer.			
11. Removes resident's garment from one arm.			
12. Dries underarm with towel, if necessary.			
13. Places thermometer bulb in center of axilla.			
14. Places resident's arm across chest to hold thermometer in place.			
15. Leaves thermometer in place for 10 minutes.			
16. Never leaves resident with a thermometer in place.			
17. Removes thermometer.			
18. Disposes of thermometer sleeve.			
19. Observes mercury, and makes written note of temperature reading.			
• Writes an "A" after reading to indicate it is axillary temperature.			
20. Records reading in resident's medical chart.			
21. Perform hand hygiene.			
22. Notifies charge nurse immediately of any abnormal temperature reading.			

Procedures	Y	N	Comments
Tympanic Temperature			
1. Assembles necessary equipment:			
• tympanic thermometer			
• disposable cover			
• pen			
• paper			
2. Perform hand hygiene.			
3. Explains procedure to resident.			
4. Provides privacy for resident.			
5. Puts disposable sleeve on probe of thermometer.			
6. Has resident turn his or her head so an ear is facing self.			
7. Inserts probe gently.			
8. Pulls down and back on earlobe so probe can enter ear more easily.			
9. Removes probe when instrument buzzes or flashes a light to indicate reading is complete.			
10. Observes display screen.			
11. Makes written note of temperature reading.			
• Writes a "T" after reading to indicate it is tympanic temperature.			
12. Records reading in resident's medical chart.			
13. Discards cover.			
14. Returns tympanic thermometer to charging unit.			
15. Perform hand hygiene.			
16. Notifies charge nurse immediately of any abnormal temperature reading.			

Procedures	Y	N	Comments
PULSE			
Taking a Radial Pulse			
1. Assembles necessary equipment:			
• watch with a second hand			
• pen			
• paper			
2. Perform hand hygiene.			
3. Explains procedure to resident.			
4. Positions resident's arm so that it is supported and comfortable.			
5. Places own middle fingers on palm side of resident's wrist in line with thumb.			
6. Presses gently to feel pulse. Pressing too hard may stop flow of blood.			
7. Does not use own thumb to check pulse as thumb has its own pulse and will confuse measurement.			
8. When pulse has been located, notes rhythm of beats.			
• Is it steady or irregular?			
• Is force of beat strong or weak?			
9. If pulse is steady, takes 30-second reading.			
10. Notes position of second hand on watch.			
• Counts pulse beats for 30 seconds.			
11. Multiplies this number by two to give pulse measurement for one minute.			
12. If required by facility or any abnormalities noted, counts beats for full 60 seconds.			
13. Makes written note of pulse rate.			
14. Transfers this information to resident's medical record.			
15. Perform hand hygiene.			

Procedures	Y	N	Comments
16. Notifies charge nurse immediately if any of following conditions are observed:			
• A change in rate, force, or rhythm from previous measurement.			
• A pulse rate of over 90 or under 60 beats per minute.			
• An irregular rhythm.			
• A weak or racing pulse.			
Taking an Apical Pulse			
1. Assembles necessary equipment:			
• stethoscope			
• alcohol wipes			
• a watch with a second hand			
• pen			
• paper			
2. Perform hand hygiene.			
3. Explains procedure to resident.			
4. Provides privacy for resident.			
5. Cleans earpieces and diaphragm of stethoscope with alcohol wipes.			
6. Puts earpieces into own ears.			
7. Uncovers left side of resident's chest.			
8. Places bell or diaphragm of stethoscope on left side of chest, below nipple.			
9. When loudest sounds of heart beat located, counts beats for a full minute.			
10. Makes written note of apical pulse rate.			
11. Makes note of any irregular heart sounds noticed.			
12. Transfers information to resident's medical record.			
13. Perform hand hygiene.			

Procedures	Y	N	Comments
14. Notifies charge nurse immediately if any of following conditions are observed:			
• A change in rate, force, or rhythm from previous measurement.			
• A pulse rate of over 90 or under 60 beats per minute.			
• An irregular rhythm.			
• A weak or racing pulse.			
BLOOD PRESSURE **Taking a Blood Pressure Reading** 1. Assembles necessary equipment:			
• blood pressure cuff (sphygmomanometer)			
• stethoscope			
• alcohol wipes			
• pen			
• paper			
2. Perform hand hygiene.			
3. Explains procedure to resident.			
4. Provides privacy for resident.			
5. Resident may be either lying down or sitting up.			
6. Removes or rolls up resident's sleeve and rests forearm on bed or chair arm.			
7. Unrolls blood pressure cuff			
• loosens valve on bulb			
• squeezes cuff to release any air			
8. Cleans earpieces and diaphragm of stethoscope with alcohol wipes.			
9. Places cuff snugly around resident's arm one inch above elbow, with arrows on cuff pointing toward elbow.			
10. Locates brachial pulse (inside elbow) with own three middle fingertips.			
11. Places diaphragm of stethoscope on brachial pulse, but not touching cuff.			

Procedures	Y	N	Comments
12. Puts earpieces of stethoscope in own ears.			
13. Turns thumbscrew of valve clockwise to tighten it, being careful not to turn it too tightly.			
14. Holding stethoscope diaphragm in place over brachial artery, repeatedly squeezes bulb to inflate cuff until pulse no longer audible. This should be when mercury reaches 30 mm beyond point where pulse last heard.			
15. Slowly turns thumbscrew on valve counter-clockwise, allowing air to escape. After a few seconds, pulse should become audible again.			
16. Notes point on scale where first sound heard. This is systolic reading.			
17. Allows air to continue to escape. When sounds change or disappear, notes point on scale. This is diastolic reading.			
18. Deflates cuff completely.			
19. Removes cuff from resident's arm.			
20. Removes stethoscope from own ears.			
21. Records person's name and blood pressure on own notes.			
22. Returns equipment to proper place.			
23. Perform hand hygiene.			
24. Reports blood pressure and any abnormalities observed to charge nurse.			
RESPIRATION			
1. When charting respiration, notes and records following things:			
• Rate. How many respirations per minute?			
• Rhythm. Is rhythm regular or irregular?			
• Character. Is respiration slow, fast, noisy, or irregular.			
• Color of skin. Does skin appear unusually pink or blue?			

Checked by: _____

Date signed off *(meets all criteria)*:_____

Chapter 32 Checklists:
The Environment of Care: Resident Safety

Name: _____   Date: _____

Procedures	Y	N	Comments
Using a Fire Extinguisher			
1. Pull the fire alarm.			
2. Set the fire extinguisher upright.			
3. Remove the safety latch.			
4. Point the nozzle low at the base of the fire.			
5. Push down on the handle and water or foam will come out.			

Checked by: _____

Date signed off *(meets all criteria)*:_____

Chapter 33 Skills Checklists:
Moving a Resident

Name: _____   Date: _____

Procedures	Y	N	Comments
Moving a Resident in Bed			
1. Explains procedure to resident.			
2. Perform hand hygiene.			
3. Places resident's pillow upright on headboard to protect resident's head from injury.			
4. Stands next to bed with own feet about 12 inches apart, pointing foot closer to head of bed in that direction.			
5. Places one hand under resident's shoulders and one under buttocks.			
6. Asks resident to bend knees and brace his or her feet firmly against mattress.			
7. Upon count of "three," supports and moves resident as he or she pushes toward head of bed with feet.			
8. Remembers to keep own back straight and knees bent.			
9. Perform hand hygiene.			
Moving a Resident with a Lift Sheet			
1. Asks for help from another healthcare worker.			
2. Explains procedure to resident.			
3. Perform hand hygiene.			
4. Places resident's pillow upright on headboard to protect resident's head from injury.			
5. With one person on each side of bed, rolls both sides of lift sheet as close as possible to resident's body.			
6. Stands straight, with own feet 12 inches apart and pointed in direction of move. Keeps own body turned slightly toward head of bed.			

Procedures	Y	N	Comments
7. Grasps rolled sheet at resident's shoulders and hip. Asks resident to raise his or her head on count of "three."			
8. Counts "One, two, three . . . lift," and then lifts.			
9. When lifting, keeps own back straight and own knees bent.			
10. Shifts own weight from one foot to other while supporting resident.			
11. Perform hand hygiene when finished.			
Moving a Resident Without a Lift Sheet			
1. Explains procedure to resident.			
2. Perform hand hygiene.			
3. With own hands under resident's knees and ankles, moves resident's feet and legs toward self.			
4. Places own forearms under resident's small of back and buttocks and moves resident toward self.			
5. Places own hands under resident's shoulders and moves resident toward self.			
6. Supports resident's back with pillow when resident lying on his or her side.			
7. Perform hand hygiene when finished.			
Turning a Resident Away from You			
1. Explains procedure to resident.			
2. Perform hand hygiene.			
3. With own hand under resident's knees and ankles, moves resident's feet and legs toward self.			
4. Places own forearms under resident's small of back and buttocks and moves resident toward self.			
5. Places own hands under resident's shoulders and moves resident toward self.			
6. If possible, bends resident's knee nearest self. If knee cannot be bent, crosses near leg over far leg.			

Procedures	Y	N	Comments
7. Places one hand on knee and one on hip.			
8. Rolls resident over.			
9. Moves own hand from knees to hips and from hips to shoulder to complete turn.			
10. Supports resident's back with pillow.			
11. Perform hand hygiene when finished.			
Turning a Resident Toward You			
1. Explains procedure to resident.			
2. Perform hand hygiene.			
3. Crosses leg farthest away over leg closest.			
4. Crosses resident's arms over chest.			
5. Reaches across resident and puts one hand behind shoulder.			
6. Places own other hand behind resident's hip and gently rolls resident toward self.			
7. Supports resident's back with pillow.			
8. Perform hand hygiene when finished			
Turning a Resident Using The Log-Rolling Technique			
1. Asks another health care worker for help.			
2. Explains procedure to resident.			
3. Perform hand hygiene.			
4. Rolls a lift sheet as close as possible to both sides of resident's body.			
5. Coordinates movements by counting.			
6. Lifts and moves resident to one side of bed while keeping knees bent and back straight.			
7. Uses lift sheet to roll resident onto his or her side.			
8. Turns body as one unit without bending resident's joints, while helper supports resident's legs.			
9. Makes sure resident in correct body alignment.			
10. Positions pillows properly for support.			
11. Perform hand hygiene before leaving resident.			

Procedures	Y	N	Comments
Pivot Transfer from Bed to Wheelchair			
1. Explains procedure to resident.			
2. Perform hand hygiene.			
3. Makes sure resident wearing shoes with nonskid soles.			
4. Positions wheelchair on resident's non-paralyzed side.			
5. Places chair at 45 degree angle to bed with brakes locked and pedals up.			
6. Helps resident sit on edge of bed with legs and feet hanging over edge.			
7. Puts gait belt on resident.			
8. Stands in front of resident and firmly grasps gait belt in hands.			
9. Ensures that resident has his or her arms at own waist, and not around own neck.			
10. Stands so own feet are about 18 inches apart and so resident's paralyzed or weakened leg is between own knees.			
11. Helps resident stand, supporting paralyzed leg with own knees.			
12. Has resident use non-paralyzed hand to grasp wheelchair armrest.			
13. Pivots own body, helping resident to pivot toward non-paralyzed leg.			
14. Bends own knees, keeping own back straight, and helps resident sit in chair.			
15. Perform hand hygiene when finished.			
Transferring the Dependent Resident			
1. Explains procedure to resident.			
2. Perform hand hygiene.			
3. Places wheelchair at 45 degree angle to bed and facing foot of bed.			
4. Locks brakes of wheelchair.			

Procedures	Y	N	Comments
5. Taller person should be at head of bed and shorter at resident's knees.			
6. Helps resident sit up in bed, keeping legs and feet on bed.			
7. Nursing assistant at head reaches around resident, crosses resident's arms, and grasps wrists.			
8. Other person reaches under resident's knees and thighs.			
9. On count of "three," lifts and moves residents to edge of bed.			
10. Adjusts base of support.			
11. On count of "three," lifts resident into wheelchair, keeping own back straight and knees bent.			
12. Perform hand hygiene when finished.			
Using a Mechanical Lift			
1. Asks another healthcare worker for help.			
2. Explains procedure to resident.			
3. Perform hand hygiene.			
4. Places wheelchair next to bed with back of chair in line with headboard.			
5. Turns resident from side to side on bed while sliding sling under resident.			
6. Attaches slings to mechanical lift with hooks in place through metal frame.			
7. Has resident fold both arms across chest, if possible.			
8. Lifts resident out of bed by turning crank.			
9. Has other healthcare worker guide resident's legs.			
10. Lowers resident into wheelchair.			
11. Removes hooks from frame.			
12. Leaves sling under resident for use when lifting him or her back into bed.			

Procedures	Y	N	Comments
13. Perform hand hygiene when finished.			
Completing a Transfer or Positioning			
1. Makes sure call bell is within resident's reach.			
2. Makes sure side rails of bed are up.			
3. Makes sure bed is lowered to its lowest position.			
4. Thanks resident for cooperating.			
5. Perform hand hygiene.			

Checked by: _____

Date signed off *(meets all criteria)*:_____

Chapter 34 Skills Checklists:
Ambulation

Name: _____   Date: _____

Procedures	Y	N	Comments
ASSISTING AMBULATION			
1. Explains procedure to resident.			
2. Tells resident what he or she is expected to do.			
3. Perform hand hygiene.			
4. Helps resident sit up.			
5. Allows time for resident to gain his or her balance.			
6. Fastens gait belt around resident's waist.			
7. Helps resident put on firm shoes.			
8. Firmly grasps both sides of gait belt to help resident stand up and maintain his or her balance.			
9. Stands on unaffected (strong) side, and helps resident stand up.			
10. Remembers to keep own back straight.			
11. Allows time for resident to gain balance, but doesn't let go of gait belt.			
12. Reminds resident to stand as straight as possible with chin parallel to floor.			
13. Walks along with resident, providing support with gait belt.			
14. Remains alert to signs of fatigue, such as rapid breathing, rapid heartbeat, sweating, or dizziness.			
15. If these are observed, stops and helps resident sit or lie down.			
16. Remains alert to hazards, such as spills, items on floor, or untied shoelaces.			
17. Returns resident to chair or bed.			
18. Removes gait belt.			
19. Perform hand hygiene.			
20. In resident's medical chart, notes distance, time ambulated, and resident's response.			

Checked by: _____

Date signed off *(meets all criteria)*: _____

Chapter 35 Skills Checklists:
Safety in Ambulation and Restraint

Name: _____   Date: _____

Procedures	Y	N	Comments
Identification			
1. Calls patient by name, but does not rely on this alone for identification.			
2. Compares name on identification bracelet to any order for treatment. Every resident should have an ID bracelet that lists:			
• name			
• room number and bed			
• age			
• sex			
• doctor's name			
• any allergies			
3. If any doubt at all, double checks with charge nurse before providing care.			
Side Rails			
1. Before raising or lowering side rails, checks to be sure resident's arms and legs are out of way.			
2. Securely locks side rails into position, whether up or down.			
3. Never ties restraints to side rails.			
4. Reports broken side rails immediately to charge nurse.			
5. Uses side rail padding to prevent injury to residents who thrash about in bed.			
Wheelchair			
1. Always locks brakes before attempting to transfer resident into or out of wheelchair.			
2. Ensures that footrests are up when resident is transferring into or out of wheelchair.			

Procedures	Y	N	Comments
3. Footrests should be down for support for feet when resident sitting in wheelchair.			
4. Keeps resident's limbs and clothing away from wheels.			
5. Immediately reports broken or defective parts to charge nurse.			
6. Uses care during wheelchair transfers. Older residents have fragile skin which injures easily.			
7. When moving resident in wheelchair, remains alert to obstacles and hazards.			
Walker			
1. Checks walker regularly and immediately reports any broken or defective parts.			
2. Keeps resident's path free of obstacles and hazards.			
3. If resident appears to be using walker improperly, reports this to charge nurse immediately.			
4. If walker appears to be wrong size for resident, checks with physical therapist or charge nurse immediately.			
Crutches			
1. Checks underarm padding to be sure it is adequate and in good repair.			
2. Makes sure there are no loose screws and tips are in good repair.			
3. Checks resident's underarm area for signs of pressure.			
• If found, notifies charge nurse immediately.			
4. If resident appears to be having difficulty or uses crutches improperly, notifies charge nurse immediately.			

Procedures	Y	N	Comments
Cane			
1. Check cane regularly for loose screws or cracks.			
2. Rubber tips should be clean and in good repair.			
3. Reports to charge nurse any difficulty resident has using cane.			
SOFT PROTECTIVE DEVICES			
The Use Of Restraints			
1. Approaches resident in calm, unhurried manner.			
2. Makes sure physician's orders are present.			
3. Makes sure that it is the correct resident.			
4. Perform hand hygiene.			
5. Explains procedure to resident and his or her family in a simple, non-threatening way.			
6. Stresses protective purpose of supports, using non-threatening terms such as "safety belt" and "postural support."			
7. Only uses restraints when resident is in bed or chair which has wheels. If there is an emergency, resident will have to be moved quickly.			
8. Never ties restraints to side rails or parts of bed that are raised or lowered. If rails or parts of bed were raised or lowered with limb attached, restraint might injure resident.			
9. Ties restraints in simple, easy-to-release knots placed out of resident's reach.			
• Never uses slip knot as it can tighten when resident moves.			
10. Checks resident for proper positioning before restraint is applied.			
11. Restraints, when in place, should fit snugly, without binding. Checks to see if two fingers can be slipped under edge of restraint after it has been tied.			

Procedures	Y	N	Comments
12. Restraints must never restrict resident's circulation.			
13. Checks resident for following signs of restricted circulation:			
• change in skin color			
• change in skin temperature			
• complaints of tingling, numbness, or pain			
• swelling			
14. Protects resident's skin from wrinkles, knots, and buckles. Uses padded restraints or pads bony places to prevent pressure sores.			
15. Observes resident in supportive restraints every hour.			
16. Observes resident in treatment restraints every 15 minutes or as required by Policies and Procedures of facility.			
17. Enters observations in Nurse's Notes at end of each shift.			
18. Releases restraints every one to two hours for short periods, to allow for massage, exercise and movement. This also provides time for a position change.			
19. Ensures that resident is able to reach and use call button.			
20. Never uses restraints as punishment or for convenience of staff.			

Checked by: _____

Date signed off *(meets all criteria)*:_____

Chapter 36 Skills Checklists:
Inactivity and Range of Motion Exercises

Name: _____   Date: _____

Procedures	Y	N	Comments
Passive Range of Motion Exercises			
1. Explains procedure to resident.			
2. Perform hand hygiene.			
3. Provides privacy for resident.			
4. Places resident in supine position with knees extended and arms at side.			
5. Raises side rail on far side of bed.			
6. Exercises resident's neck.			
7. Remembers to never move resident's joint past point of pain throughout all exercises.			
8. Exercises each shoulder.			
9. Exercises each elbow.			
10. Exercises each wrist.			
11. Exercises each finger.			
12. Exercises each hip.			
13. Exercises each knee.			
14. Exercises each ankle.			
15. Exercises each toe.			
16. Perform hand hygiene.			
17. Charts the following:			
• time			
• exercises performed			
• whether active or passive			
• any abnormalities			
• any complaints			
18. Reports any abnormalities or complaints to charge nurse.			

Checked by: _____

Date signed off *(meets all criteria)*:_____

Chapter 37 Skills Checklists:
Pressure Ulcers and Positioning

Name: _____ Date: _____

Procedures	Y	N	Comments
Supine Position - Lying on Back			
1. Explains procedure to resident.			
2. Perform hand hygiene.			
3. Places pillow under head and slightly under shoulders.			
4. Avoids using two pillows as this can lead to neck contractures and pain.			
5. Places resident's arms away from body to allow air circulation in axilla (armpit).			
• Alternates between palms up and palms down.			
6. Prevents or lessens hand contractures by placing small towel or piece of foam rubber in resident's hand to prevent fist closure.			
7. Places resident's legs slightly apart to allow air circulation in perineal area.			
8. Prevents legs from rotating outward by placing rolled towel or blanket at hip joint.			
9. Places feet flat against a padded foot board to prevent foot drop, a contracture that occurs in residents who are bed-ridden.			
10. Places small rolled towel or small piece of foam rubber under resident's heels to elevate and prevent pressure on heels.			
11. Use of foot cradle can prevent additional pressure from bedding.			
12. Changes resident to another position every two hours.			
13. Perform hand hygiene when finished.			
Semi-supine Position			
1. Explains procedure to resident.			
2. Perform hand hygiene.			

Procedures	Y	N	Comments
3. Rolls resident toward self.			
4. Places one pillow behind resident's back for support.			
5. Places another pillow under resident's top leg, level with hip joint.			
6. Confirms that both legs are straight with top leg a little behind bottom leg and supported by pillow.			
7. Checks lower shoulder placement, and ensures that it is forward so that pressure is distributed over back of shoulder rather than on one shoulder.			
8. Perform hand hygiene when finished.			
9. Changes resident to another position every two hours.			
Prone Position - Lying on Stomach			
1. Explains procedure to resident.			
2. Perform hand hygiene.			
3. Rolls resident over onto stomach.			
4. Turns head to one side without pillow.			
5. Aligns body with spine straight.			
6. Checks to see if resident will be more comfortable with a flat pillow under abdomen.			
7. Places shoulder rolls lengthwise under each shoulder if shoulders tend to roll forward.			
8. Positions both arms down at side, or one down and one flexed up, whichever is more comfortable.			
9. Avoids flexing both arms up, as this puts strain on shoulders.			
10. Positions feet so that toes fall between mattress and footboard of bed.			
11. Places rolled towel under ankles to relieve pressure on toes or top of foot as needed.			
12. Perform hand hygiene when finished.			
13. Changes resident to another position every two hours.			

Procedures	Y	N	Comments
Side-lying Position			
1. Explains procedure to resident.			
2. Perform hand hygiene.			
3. From prone position, lifts resident's shoulder closest to self and places pillow under chest and shoulder with arm over pillow.			
4. Positions other arm behind resident.			
5. Place a second pilow lengthwise under the top leg, making certain that the knees are slightly flexed.			
6. Confirms that one leg is positioned in front of the other.			
7. Perform hand hygiene when finished.			
8. Changes resident to another position every two hours.			
Completing a Transfer or Positioning			
1. Ensures that call bell is within resident's reach.			
2. Ensures that side rails of bed are up.			
3. Ensures that bed is lowered to its lowest position.			
4. Thanks resident for cooperating.			
5. Perform hand hygiene.			

Checked by: _____

Date signed off *(meets all criteria)*:_____

Chapter 38 Skills Checklists:
Bedmaking and Comfort Measures

Name: _____   Date: _____

Procedures	Y	N	Comments
BEDMAKING			
Making An Unoccupied Bed			
1. Removes soiled linens.			
2. Places in dirty linen container.			
3. Perform hand hygiene.			
4. Obtains clean linens.			
5. Adjusts bed to comfortable working height to protect own back.			
6. Unfolds clean bottom sheet lengthwise on bed.			
• Starting at foot of bed, opens sheet.			
• Makes sure sheet hangs evenly on each side of bed.			
• Makes sure that hem at foot of bed is even with end of mattress.			
• Raises mattress and tucks in sheet at head.			
• Miters corner.			
• Picks up edge of sheet to make triangle.			
• Lays triangle on top of bed.			
• Tucks hanging portion under mattress.			
• Holds fold at edge of mattress.			
• Miters corner by bringing triangle down and tucking it under mattress.			
• Tucks hanging portion of sheet all the way to foot of bed.			
7. Places draw sheet across bottom sheet.			
• Tucks draw sheet under mattress.			
8. Lays top sheet lengthwise on bed.			
• Leaves enough sheet at head of bed to fold over top of bedspread later.			
• Spread sheet so it hangs evenly on each side of bed.			

Procedures	Y	N	Comments
9. Lays bedspread and/or blanket over top sheet.			
• Opens it so that it hangs evenly on each side of bed.			
10. Folds hem of top sheet over top covers.			
11. Tucks top covers together at foot of bed.			
12. Miters corners without tucking them under mattress.			
13. Moves to other side of bed.			
14. Makes triangle tuck in bottom sheet at head.			
15. Then miters corners of sheet.			
16. Tucks in hanging portion of bottom sheet and drawsheet.			
17. Miters top covers at foot of bed.			
18. Forms toe pleat at foot of bed.			
19. Grasps both sides of top covers at mitered corners and gently pulls enough of covers toward foot to make a three or four inch fold at foot of bed, thereby preventing pressure on resident's toes.			
20. Holds pillowcase at center of end seam.			
21. Turns pillowcase back over own hand.			
22. Grasps end of pillow right through pillowcase.			
• Brings pillowcase down over pillow.			
• Fits corners of pillow into seamless corners of pillowcase.			
• Folds extra material from side seam under pillow.			
23. Places pillow on bed with open end away from door.			
24. Places call signal in position.			
25. Returns bed to its lowest position.			
26. Perform hand hygiene when finished.			

Procedures	Y	N	Comments
Making An Occupied Bed			
1. Assembles clean linens on bedside chair.			
2. Explains procedure to resident.			
3. Perform hand hygiene.			
4. Provides privacy for resident.			
5. Raises bed to comfortable working height.			
6. Brings backrest and knee rest to flat position.			
7. Loosens bed covers all around bed.			
8. Leaves top covers over resident for warmth and privacy.			
9. Raises side rail for protection of resident before going to opposite side.			
10. Turns resident on his or her side.			
11. Makes sure pillow supports resident's head.			
12. Changes bottom sheet and draw sheet:			
• Rolls used draw sheet and full width of bottom sheet against resident's back and legs and tucks it there.			
• Unfolds fresh bottom sheet with its lengthwise center fold along center of bed.			
• Bottom hem should be even with mattress.			
• Places draw sheet over bottom sheet.			
• Tucks against resident's back.			
• Tucks bottom sheet at head of mattress.			
• Miters top corner.			
• Drops side and tucks in bottom sheet and draw sheet all along side of bed.			
• Raises side rail where work done and goes around to other side of bed.			
• Lowers other side rail.			
• Rolls resident onto fresh bottom sheet and draw sheet.			
• Removes soiled bottom sheet and soiled draw sheet.			

Procedures	Y	N	Comments
• Maintains resident's privacy.			
• Puts soiled linen into soiled linen hamper.			
• Pulls clean bottom sheet and draw sheet toward self.			
• Tightens sheets, making them as wrinkle-free as possible.			
• Miters top corner same as other side.			
• Tucks in bottom sheet.			
• Draws sheet all along side of bed.			
• Rolls resident onto his or her back.			
13. Spreads clean top sheet over resident.			
• Removes blanket or bedspread.			
• Asks resident to hold onto fresh top sheet, if possible.			
• Pulls soiled top sheet out from under it.			
• Places blanket or bedspread over resident.			
• Tucks in top covers.			
• Miters corners at foot of bed.			
• Forms toe pleat at foot of bed.			
• Grasps both sides of top covers at mitered corners and gently pulls enough of covers toward foot to make a three or four inch fold at foot of bed, thereby preventing pressure on resident's toes.			
14. Changes pillowcase.			
• Holds pillowcase at center of end seam.			
• Turns case back over own hand.			
• Grasps end of pillow right through pillowcase.			
• Brings pillowcase down over pillow and fits corners of pillow into seamless corners of pillowcase.			
• Folds extra material from side seam under pillow.			
15. Places pillow on bed with open end away from door.			

Procedures	Y	N	Comments
16. Returns bed to its lowest position.			
17. Makes sure side rails are up before moving away from resident.			
18. Lowers bed.			
19. Raises head of bed.			
20. Places call signal within reach.			
21. Makes sure resident is comfortable.			
22. Perform hand hygiene when finished.			
COMFORT MEASURES **Back Rub** 1. Assembles necessary equipment:			
• lotion			
• basin of warm water (105 degrees F)			
• towel			
2. Explains procedure to resident.			
3. Perform hand hygiene.			
4. Provides privacy for resident.			
5. Places bottle of lotion in pan of warm water.			
6. Positions resident so that his or her back is toward self, or resident is lying face down.			
7. Places towel lengthwise on bed next to resident's back.			
8. Pours small amounts of lotion into palm of own hand.			
9. Rubs own hands together to warm hands and lotion.			
10. Applies lotion with long, firm strokes upward from buttocks to back of neck and shoulders.			
11. Strokes upward using firm pressure and downward using gentle pressure, using circular motion over bony areas.			
12. Ensures that hands never leave resident's back, as this can create shocks to resident.			

Procedures	Y	N	Comments
13. Uses one continuous flowing motion.			
14. Continues for three minutes.			
15. Pats resident's back with towel.			
16. Assists resident with dressing.			
17. Positions resident comfortably.			
18. Perform hand hygiene when finished.			
Perineal Care			
1. Assembles necessary equipment:			
• disposable bed protector			
• bedpan			
• basin			
• peri-wash solution (if used by facility)			
• soap			
• two washcloths			
• towels			
2. Explains procedure to resident.			
3. Perform hand hygiene.			
4. Provides privacy for resident.			
5. Offers resident bedpan or urinal.			
6. Places disposable bed protector under resident's buttocks.			
7. Assists resident onto bedpan.			
8. Puts on protective gloves before continuing.			
9. Positions resident's legs apart.			
10. Sprays peri-wash solution over resident's perineal area.			
11. Uses wet washcloth to clean area.			
12. Rinses washcloth.			
13. Wipes solution from perineal area.			

Procedures	Y	N	Comments
14. Observes resident's skin for any rashes or sores.			
• For female residents, spreads labia and washes from front to back.			
• For uncircumcised males, retracts foreskin and washes head of penis thoroughly.			
• If resident is soiled with urine or feces, uses soap and water before using peri-wash solution.			
15. Dries area with soft towel.			
16. Removes bedpan and disposable bed protector.			
17. Discards bed protector and gloves according to policies of facility.			
18. Empties equipment.			
19. Rinses and cleans equipment used.			
20. Deposits soiled linen in soiled linen container.			
21. Perform hand hygiene when finished.			

Checked by: _____

Date signed off *(meets all criteria)*:_____

Chapter 39 Skills Checklists:
Bathing the Resident

Name: _____   Date: _____

Procedures	Y	N	Comments
TYPES OF BATHS			
Shower			
1. Assembles bathing equipment on shelf or regular chair near shower:			
• towel			
• soap			
• wash cloth			
• shower cap			
• clean clothing			
2. Takes shower chair and large sheets to resident's bedside.			
3. Explains procedure to resident.			
4. Perform hand hygiene.			
5. Provides privacy for resident.			
6. Removes resident's clothes.			
7. Transfers resident to shower chair, making sure wheels are locked.			
8. Covers resident, making sure that entire body including buttock area and limbs are covered.			
9. Unlocks wheels and quickly transports resident to shower area.			
10. Turns on water.			
11. Adjusts temperature of water.			
12. Gives resident soap and wash cloth and encourages resident to wash and rinse as much as possible. Assists when necessary.			
13. Puts on gloves if washing perineal area or face.			
14. Turns off water.			
15. Assists resident in drying thoroughly.			
16. Assists resident with dressing.			

Procedures	Y	N	Comments
17. Returns to shower and cleans it.			
18. Removes any soiled linen from shower.			
19. Disposes of gloves, if used.			
20. Perform hand hygiene.			
Tub Bath			
1. Assembles bathing equipment on chair near tub:			
• towel			
• soap			
• wash cloth			
• clean clothing			
2. Explains procedure to resident.			
3. Perform hand hygiene.			
4. Provides privacy for resident.			
5. Fills tub half full with water at 105 degrees F.			
6. Tests water with thermometer and inside of own wrist.			
7. Lets resident test water for comfort.			
8. Places towel or bath mat on floor beside tub to prevent slipping when getting out.			
9. Assists resident in removing clothing and jewelry.			
10. Assists resident into tub.			
11. Gives resident soap and wash cloth.			
12. Encourages him or her to wash and rinse as much as possible.			
13. Assists when necessary.			
14. Never leaves resident alone in tub.			
15. Puts gloves on before washing perineal area or face.			
16. Assists resident out of tub, encouraging use of grab bars.			
17. Assists resident in drying thoroughly.			
18. Assists resident with dressing.			

Procedures	Y	N	Comments
19. Washes tub with disinfectant.			
20. Places soiled linen in covered dirty linen container.			
21. Disposes of gloves, if used.			
22. Perform hand hygiene.			
Complete Bed Bath			
1. Assembles necessary equipment on bedside table:			
• soap in container			
• wash cloth			
• wash basin			
• bath blanket (if available)			
2. Explains procedure to resident.			
3. Provides privacy for resident.			
4. Perform hand hygiene.			
5. Puts on gloves.			
6. Offers resident bedpan or urinal.			
7. Removes and folds bedspread and blankets.			
8. Covers resident with bath blanket or top sheet.			
9. Lowers head and foot of bed to flat position and raises entire bed to comfortable working height.			
10. Ensures that side rail on opposite side is up.			
11. Positions resident comfortably for bath.			
12. Assists resident in moving closer to self.			
13. Removes resident's clothing and jewelry.			
14. Keeps resident covered to prevent chilling.			
15. Fills wash basin two-thirds full with water at 105 degrees F.			
16. Tests it with thermometer and on inside of own wrist.			
17. Lets resident test water for comfort.			
18. Lays towel across resident's chest.			
19. Makes mitt with wash cloth.			

Procedures	Y	N	Comments
20. Begins by washing eyes from nose to outside of face, using only water unless otherwise requested.			
21. Rinses and dries face by patting gently with towel.			
22. Places towel lengthwise under arm farthest from self.			
23. Supports arm with own hand under resident's elbow.			
• Washes shoulder, axilla, and arm with mild soap or special bathing preparation.			
• Rinses and dries well.			
• Places basin of water on towel.			
• Places resident's hand into water.			
• Washes, rinses, and dries hand.			
24. Places towel lengthwise under arm nearest to self.			
25. Supports arm with own hand under resident's elbow.			
• Washes shoulder, axilla, and arm with mild soap or special bathing preparation.			
• Rinses and dries well.			
• Places basin of water on towel.			
• Places resident's hand into water.			
• Washes, rinses, and dries hand.			
26. Folds sheet down to resident's abdomen.			
27. Washes resident's:			
• ears			
• neck			
• chest (for female residents, lifts breasts to wash thoroughly)			
28. Rinses resident's:			
• ears			
• neck			
• chest (for female residents, lifts breasts to rinse thoroughly)			

Procedures	Y	N	Comments
29. Dries resident's:			
• ears			
• neck			
• chest (for female residents, lifts breasts to dry thoroughly)			
30. Covers chest with towel.			
31. Folds sheet down to pubic area.			
32. Washes, rinses, and dries resident's abdomen, being careful to include umbilicus and skin creases.			
33. Pulls sheet up over abdomen and chest.			
34. Removes towel.			
35. Empties wash basin.			
36. Rinses wash basin.			
37. Refills wash basin with clean water if it becomes soapy or cool.			
38. Makes sure that side rail is raised anytime resident left alone.			
39. Tests water for proper temperature.			
40. Folds sheet back from resident's leg farthest from self and places towel lengthwise under leg.			
• Bends knee and washes, rinses, and dries leg and foot.			
• If resident can bend knee easily, places basin on a towel.			
• Places resident's foot in water and washes it.			
• Covers resident's leg and foot with sheet.			
• Removes towel.			

Procedures	Y	N	Comments
41. Folds sheet back from resident's leg nearest self.			
• Bends knee and washes, rinses, and dries leg and foot.			
• If resident can bend knee easily, places basin on a towel.			
• Places resident's foot in water and washes it.			
• Covers resident's leg and foot with sheet.			
• Removes towel.			
42. Empties basin.			
43. Rinses basin.			
44. Refills basin with clean water.			
45. Tests for proper temperature.			
46. Assists resident to turn on his or her side so back is toward self.			
47. Places towel lengthwise on bed near resident's back.			
48. Washes resident's:			
• back of neck			
• behind ears			
• back			
• buttocks			
49. Rinses resident's:			
• back of neck			
• behind ears			
• back			
• buttocks			
50. Dries resident's:			
• back of neck			
• behind ears			
• back			
• buttocks			
51. Removes towel.			
52. Assists resident in turning onto his or her back.			

Procedures	Y	N	Comments
53. Empties basin, rinses and refills with clear water.			
54. Tests water for proper temperature.			
55. If resident able to wash his or her own perineal area, provides:			
• soapy washcloth			
• clean, wet cloth for rinse			
• towel to dry			
56. If resident is unable to do this, assists by washing perineal area front to back to avoid infection.			
• For female residents, spreads labia and washes front to back.			
• For uncircumcised males, retracts foreskin and washes tip of penis.			
57. Assists resident into clean clothing.			
58. Removes sheets.			
59. Remakes bed with clean linen.			
60. Disposes of gloves.			
61. Perform hand hygiene.			
Partial Bed Bath			
1. Assembles necessary equipment on bedside table:			
• soap in container			
• wash cloth			
• wash basin			
• towel			
• bath blanket (if available)			
2. Explains procedure to resident.			
3. Provides privacy for resident.			
4. Perform hand hygiene.			
5. Puts on gloves.			
6. Offers a bedpan or urinal.			
7. Removes and folds bedspread and blankets.			

Procedures	Y	N	Comments
8. Covers resident with top sheet or bath blanket if available.			
9. Assists resident in removing clothing and jewelry.			
10. Fills basin two-thirds full with water at 105 degrees F.			
11. Tests water with thermometer.			
12. Tests water with inside of own wrist.			
13. Asks resident to test temperature for comfort.			
14. Asks resident to wash areas of body which he or she can easily reach.			
15. Asks resident to signal with call light when finished.			
16. Disposes of gloves.			
17. Perform hand hygiene.			
18. Leaves resident to continue bathing.			
19. When resident signals, returns to room.			
20. Perform hand hygiene.			
21. Puts on gloves.			
22. Empties basin.			
23. Rinses basin.			
24. Refills basin with clean water.			
25. Tests it for proper temperature.			
26. Washes areas of body resident unable to reach, following procedures outlined in Complete Bed Bath above.			
27. Rinses areas of body resident unable to reach, following procedures outlined in Complete Bed Bath above.			
28. Dries areas of body resident unable to reach, following procedures outlined in Complete Bed Bath above.			
29. Assists resident in putting on clean clothing.			
30. Removes sheets.			
31. Remakes bed with clean linen.			
32. Disposes of gloves.			
33. Perform hand hygiene.			

Checked by: _____

Date signed off *(meets all criteria)*:_____

The New Nursing Assistant
Skills Checklists

Chapter 40 Skills Checklists:
Personal Hygiene

Name: _____   Date: _____

Procedures	Y	N	Comments
Residents Who Still Have Their Teeth			
1. Explains procedure to resident.			
2. Perform hand hygiene.			
3. Puts on gloves.			
4. Assists resident in using bathroom sink if possible.			
5. If resident is in bed, places towel on resident's chest.			
6. Places emesis basin under resident's chin.			
7. Uses dry, soft bristle, junior size toothbrush held at 45 degree angle to teeth.			
• Stimulates gums by brushing in circular motion where teeth and gums meet.			
• Begins with upper teeth and gums.			
• Does lower teeth and gums.			
8. Places toothpaste on toothbrush.			
• Stimulates gums by brushing in circular motion where teeth and gums meet.			
• Begins with upper teeth and gums, brushing first outer surfaces, then inner and chewing surfaces.			
• Does lower teeth and gums, brushing first outer surfaces, then inner and chewing surfaces.			
9. Has resident rinse his or her mouth with warm water.			
10. Has resident expectorate, or spit water out into emesis basin if in bed.			
11. If mouthwash used, dilutes with four parts water to one part mouthwash.			
12. Puts all personal items away in resident's drawer.			
13. Disposes of gloves.			
14. Perform hand hygiene.			

Procedures	Y	N	Comments
Residents With Dentures			
1. Explains procedure to resident.			
2. Perform hand hygiene.			
3. Puts on gloves.			
4. If resident is in bed, places a towel on resident's chest.			
5. Places an emesis basin under resident's chin.			
6. Places paper towels in bottom of sink to protect dentures from accidental breakage if dropped.			
7. If resident is able, asks him or her to remove dentures.			
8. If resident requires assistance, removes dentures gently.			
• Removes upper plate by pushing down gently to break suction.			
9. Puts dentures in basin.			
10. Takes basin to sink.			
11. Brushes dentures with toothpaste.			
12. Rinses dentures under running water.			
13. Places dentures in clean, rinsed denture cup.			
14. Encourages resident to rinse his or her mouth with diluted mouthwash (one part mouthwash to four parts water).			
15. Replaces dentures in resident's mouth or stores them in cold water in denture cup.			
16. Disposes of gloves.			
17. Perform hand hygiene.			

Procedures	Y	N	Comments
Shampooing			
1. Assembles necessary equipment:			
• brush			
• comb			
• shampoo			
• creme rinse			
• towel			
2. Explains procedure to resident.			
3. Perform hand hygiene.			
4. Gently brushes hair to loosen dirt and tangles.			
5. Asks resident to do this if he or she is able.			
6. Wets resident's hair.			
7. Applies shampoo to wet hair.			
8. Washes thoroughly, being careful to keep shampoo out of resident's eyes.			
9. Rinses thoroughly, while protecting resident's eyes.			
10. Applies creme rinse to prevent tangles.			
11. Rinses resident's hair thoroughly.			
12. Dries hair with towel.			
13. Has resident assist if possible.			
14. Washes resident's comb and brush.			
15. Stores resident's comb and brush appropriately.			
16. Perform hand hygiene when finished.			

Procedures	Y	N	Comments
Shaving			
1. Assembles necessary equipment:			
• a basin of warm water (115 degrees F)			
• shaving cream			
• safety razor			
• towel			
• washcloth			
• aftershave			
2. Perform hand hygiene.			
3. Puts on gloves.			
4. Explains procedure to resident.			
5. Places towel under resident's chin.			
6. If resident wears dentures, ensures they are in his mouth.			
7. Puts washcloth in warm water.			
8. Wrings washcloth out.			
9. Places washcloth on face to soften beard.			
10. Applies shaving cream to face.			
11. With fingers of one hand, holds resident's skin taut.			
12. With other hand, shaves in direction hair grows.			
13. Uses short, firm strokes to shave:			
• under sideburns			
• downward over cheeks			
• over chin			
• upward on neck			
14. Rinses razor often.			
15. Washes remaining shaving cream off face.			
16. Applies aftershave if resident desires it.			
17. Stores all articles in appropriate place.			
18. When finished, disposes of gloves.			
19. Perform hand hygiene.			

Procedures	Y	N	Comments
NAIL CARE			
1. Assembles necessary equipment:			
• nail clippers			
• emery board			
• orange stick			
• lotion			
• basin of warm water			
• towel			
2. Perform hand hygiene.			
3. Explains procedure to resident.			
4. Places hands in basin of warm water. (If resident has just had a shower or bath, this step may be omitted.)			
5. Cleans nails with orange stick.			
6. Pushes cuticles gently back with orange stick.			
7. Dries hands.			
8. Trims nails straight across with clippers.			
9. Never uses scissors.			
10. Is very careful not to cause damage to surrounding tissue.			
11. Smoothes any rough or sharp edges with emery board.			
12. Applies lotion to resident's hands.			
13. Massages resident's hands.			
14. Perform hand hygiene when finished.			
DRESSING AND UNDRESSING			
1. Explains procedure to resident.			
2. Perform hand hygiene.			
3. Provides privacy for resident.			
4. Helps resident select clothes for day.			
5. Ensures that all buttons and hooks are undone and zippers are unzipped.			

Procedures	Y	N	Comments
6. Removes resident's nightclothes.			
7. Provides further privacy for resident with sheet, bath blanket, or bedspread.			
8. Puts underclothing on resident.			
9. Puts slacks or trousers on resident by gathering up pant leg for leg farthest from self.			
• Puts own hand up through this pant leg.			
• Grasps resident's ankle.			
• Pulls pant leg over own hand and resident's leg.			
• Repeats with other leg.			
• Pulls pants up as far as possible.			
• Has resident raise his or her hips, if possible, so that pants can be pulled up and fastened.			
• If resident is unable to do this, rolls resident to side away from self.			
• Pulls up resident's pants, and fastens them.			
10. Puts on shirts and dresses in similar way.			
• Opens shirt or dress.			
• Puts own hand backwards through sleeve farthest from self.			
• Holds resident's wrist.			
• Pulls sleeve over own hand and resident's arm.			
• Rolls resident toward self.			
• Smoothes garment across resident's back.			
• Rolls resident back.			
• Repeats steps with other sleeve.			
• Fastens garment.			
• To put on a pullover garment, places both of resident's arms in sleeves.			
• Pulls garment up on his or her arms.			
• Grasps garment neck and slides it over resident's head.			

Procedures	Y	N	Comments
• Has resident sit up, if possible, and pulls garment down.			
• If resident is unable to do this, rolls him or her from side to side while pulling garment down.			
11. Positions resident comfortably.			
12. Perform hand hygiene when finished.			

Checked by: _____

Date signed off *(meets all criteria)*:_____

Chapter 41 Skills Checklists:
Dressings and Bandages

Name: _____   Date: _____

Procedures	Y	N	Comments
DRESSINGS			
Applying a Dressing			
1. Assembles necessary equipment:			
• clean dressing			
• tape			
• scissors			
• infectious waste plastic bag			
2. Explains procedure to resident.			
3. Provides privacy for resident.			
4. Perform hand hygiene.			
5. Puts on disposable gloves.			
6. Opens dressing package, being careful not to touch dressing.			
7. Cuts strips of tape.			
8. Removes old dressing and disposes of it.			
9. *NOTE*: If old dressing shows any signs of body fluids, places in infectious waste bag for disposal.			
10. Removes gloves.			
11. Disposes of gloves.			
12. Puts on new gloves.			
13. Thoroughly cleans and dries affected area.			
14. Applies new dressing, being careful not to touch portion which will be in contact with resident's sore skin.			
15. Applies tape, covering ends of dressing. If tape is applied over a joint, places it across joint, not parallel to it.			
16. Asks nurse to dispose of bag in infectious waste container.			
17. Replaces equipment.			

Procedures	Y	N	Comments
18. Removes and disposes of gloves.			
19. Perform hand hygiene.			
20. Writes on chart that dressing has been changed.			
21. Also charts any skin abnormalities observed such as broken skin, redness, bruises, or sores.			
22. Notifies charge nurse that procedure completed, and explains any observed abnormalities.			
Elastic Bandages			
1. Selects appropriate size bandage.			
2. Explains procedure to resident.			
3. Perform hand hygiene.			
4. Provides privacy for resident.			
5. Elevates limb to be wrapped.			
6. Begins at part of limb farthest from heart.			
7. Wraps elastic bandage around limb with firm, consistent pressure.			
8. Wraps from area farthest from heart and proceeds toward heart; for example, from wrist toward elbow.			
9. Checks with resident to see if bandage is comfortable.			
10. If bandage is too tight, removes it and begins again.			
11. Perform hand hygiene when finished.			
12. Charts application of bandage.			
Elastic Stockings			
1. Selects elastic stockings of proper length and size.			
2. Explains procedure to resident.			
3. Perform hand hygiene.			
4. Provides privacy for resident.			
5. Makes sure patient is lying down.			
6. Exposes one leg at a time.			

Procedures	Y	N	Comments
7. Holds stocking at top with both hands and rolls it down to toe. (Note that any raised seams should be on outside.)			
8. Gently places rolled stocking over toes and begins to unroll.			
9. Positions toe opening at base of toes on top of foot unless toes are to remain covered.			
10. Gently unrolls stocking up leg.			
11. Ensures stocking is smooth and free of wrinkles.			
12. When stocking is applied, covers leg.			
13. Repeats procedure on opposite leg.			
14. When stockings applied to both legs, washes own hands.			
15. Charts procedure.			

Checked by: _____

Date signed off *(meets all criteria)*:_____

Chapter 42 Skills Checklists:
IV Care and Tube Feeding

Name: _____   Date: _____

Procedures	Y	N	Comments
CHANGING THE CLOTHING OF A RESIDENT ON AN IV			
1. Explains procedure to resident.			
2. Perform hand hygiene.			
3. Provides privacy for resident.			
4. Lowers bed rail, just as normally done to change resident's clothing.			
5. Unties gown or unbuttons shirt.			
• First removes gown from arm that does not have IV needle.			
• Carefully slides gown down arm that has IV needle.			
• Continues to slide gown up IV tubing to IV bottle.			
• Temporarily lifts IV bottle off its hook and slides gown over bottle.			
6. Ensures that IV bottle remains above resident.			
7. Replaces bottle on its hook.			
8. Reverses this procedure to put on new gown:			
• Temporarily lifts IV bottle off its hook.			
• Slides sleeve of new gown down over bottle.			
• Continues to slide sleeve down tubing and then onto resident's arm.			
• Puts on other sleeve and buttons or ties clothing.			
9. Makes sure IV tubing not kinked or blocked.			
10. Raises bed rails again.			
11. Perform hand hygiene when finished.			

Procedures	Y	N	Comments
TUBE FEEDING			
1. Makes sure head of bed raised.			
2. Makes sure pump working properly.			
3. Makes sure there is no alarm.			
4. Makes sure tubing not kinked.			
5. Makes sure tubing hasn't come loose.			
6. Reports any problems immediately to nurse.			

Checked by: _____

Date signed off *(meets all criteria)*:_____

Chapter 44 Skills Checklists:
Feeding a Resident

Name: _____   Date: _____

Procedures	Y	N	Comments
SERVING RESIDENTS IN DINING ROOM			
1. Perform hand hygiene.			
2. Assists resident in washing and caring for face and mouth, if needed.			
3. Assists resident to proper place in dining room.			
4. Protects resident's clothing with napkin or bib.			
5. Reminds resident of names of those sitting nearby.			
6. Encourages interaction among residents at table.			
7. Checks tray to be sure it is proper diet and meal intended for particular resident.			
8. Checks to see that resident has all necessary:			
• silverware			
• food			
• assistive eating devices if needed			
9. Perform hand hygiene.			
10. Helps resident:			
• set up tray			
• cut up food			
• butter bread			
11. Identifies food for resident.			
12. Assists only if necessary. (It is important to encourage independence in eating.)			
13. If residents can feed themselves, observes to see if they are able to complete meal.			
14. Provides assistance as needed.			
15. Knows how important it is to prevent residents from taking food from each other's plate or tray. (Certain food may not be on resident's diet.)			
16. Sits at eye level beside dependent resident when feeding him or her.			

Procedures	Y	N	Comments
17. Sits facing resident when at feeding table.			
18. When resident has finished eating, immediately writes down percentages of food eaten and fluids drunk.			
19. Transfers this information to resident's chart.			
20. Assists resident from dining room.			
21. Assists resident in:			
• performing hand hygiene			
• caring for his or her face and mouth			
22. Perform hand hygiene when finished.			
SERVING RESIDENTS IN ROOMS			
1. Explains procedure to resident.			
2. Perform hand hygiene.			
3. Assists resident to an upright position in bed or in chair.			
4. Assists resident in:			
• perform hand hygiene			
• caring for his or her face and mouth, if needed			
5. Perform hand hygiene.			
6. Protects resident's clothing or bed linen with napkin or bib.			
7. Places tray on bedside table.			
8. Checks to see that all necessary silverware and food are on tray.			
9. Verifies that resident is getting proper tray and diet.			
10. Places table in front of resident.			
11. Removes plate covers and arranges dishes and silverware so they are convenient for resident to use.			
12. If necessary:			
• identifies food for resident			
• cuts up food			
• butters bread			

Procedures	Y	N	Comments
13. Assists only as much as necessary.			
14. Encourages independent eating.			
15. If resident needs assistance in eating, sits at eye level next to resident.			
16. If resident can feed himself or herself, makes sure resident has begun eating before leaving room.			
17. When resident has finished eating, removes tray.			
18. Makes written note of percentage of each food eaten and beverages drunk.			
19. Transfers information to resident's chart.			
20. Assists resident with:			
• perform hand hygiene			
• washing face			
• mouth care			
21. Returns resident to comfortable position.			
22. Perform hand hygiene when finished.			
PROVIDING FEEDING ASSISTANCE			
1. Identifies foods on plate or tray so resident will know what he or she will be eating.			
2. Asks resident desired order for eating different foods.			
3. Perform hand hygiene.			
4. Tests temperature of food by feeling container.			
5. Tests small amount against own inner wrist. Foods that are too hot may burn a resident's mouth. Foods which are too cold may startle resident.			
6. Feeds resident using spoon.			
7. Fills spoon only half full.			
8. Places food at tip of spoon.			
9. Places food on center of resident's tongue with a slight downward pressure.			

Procedures	Y	N	Comments
10. If resident is paralyzed on one side, places food on unaffected side of tongue.			
11. Allows sufficient time for resident to chew and swallow food before putting more in mouth.			
12. Alternates solid food and fluids.			
13. If resident has difficulty drinking from a cup, uses a flexible straw.			
14. Places straw between resident's lips, not teeth.			
15. Perform hand hygiene when finished.			
THE HEIMLICH MANEUVER			
1. Stands behind resident who is standing or sitting.			
2. Places own arms around resident's waist.			
3. Makes fist with one hand.			
4. Places thumb side at point in middle of abdomen half way between resident's navel and sternum.			
5. Places other hand over own fist.			
6. Grasps own fist with other hand.			
7. Applies hard upward thrust with both hands into resident's abdomen.			
8. Performs 6 to 10 rapid abdominal thrusts like this until object expelled.			
9. When object is partially or completely dislodged, uses own fingers and sweeps resident's mouth to remove food or other material causing choking.			
10. If attempts to remove object are unsuccessful, or resident becomes unconscious, calls for assistance and begins CPR.			

Checked by: _____

Date signed off *(meets all criteria)*:_____

The New Nursing Assistant
Skills Checklists

Chapter 46 Skills Checklists:
Elimination Needs

Name: _____   Date: _____

Procedures	Y	N	Comments
CATHETER CARE			
Daily Catheter Care			
1. Assembles necessary equipment:			
• disposable bed protector			
• bedpan			
• basin of warm water (about 105° F)			
• peri-wash solution (if used by your facility)			
• soap			
• at least four washcloths, towels, bath blanket			
• protective gloves			
2. Explains procedure to resident.			
3. Provides privacy for the resident			
4. Puts on protective gloves.			
5. Offers the resident a bedpan or urinal.			
6. Places the disposable bed protector under the resident.			
7. Drapes the resident with the bath blanket, pulls bed linens to the foot of the bed.			
8. Flexes the resident's legs and position them apart.			
9. Wets washcloths, wrings out excess water.			
10. Applies soap to a wet washcloth and cleans: • Men: washes penis, scrotum and perineal area. With uncircumcised men, retracts foreskin and wash the head of the penis. • Women: spreads the labia and washes from front to back.			
11. Uses a clean wet washcloth to rinse the area.			
12. Dries the area by gently patting with a towel.			
13. Observes around the catheter for sores, crusting, leakage or bleeding. Reports any unusual observations to supervisor.			

Procedures	Y	N	Comments
14. Applies soap to new, clean, wet washcloth to clean the catheter. Starts from where the catheter leaves the body, cleans four inches of the catheter tubing. • Men: retracts foreskin of uncircumsized men. • Women: gently separates the labia with thumb and forefinger; cleans the catheter moving away from the body.			
15. Uses a clean wet washcloth to rinse the catheter.			
16. Removes the bed protector and discards it.			
17. Ensures catheter tubing is not kinked, pulling, and is not left under any part of the body.			
18. Discards protective gloves.			
19. Removes bath blanket, replaces bed linens over the resident.			
20. Makes sure resident is comfortable.			
21. Raises the side rail (if ordered by physician), leaves the call signal and personal items within reach.			
22. Empties, cleans and stores washbasin.			
23. Gathers towels and washcloths and place then in a dirty linen container according to facility's policy.			
24. Performs hand hygiene.			
Opening A Closed System			
1. Assembles necessary equipment:			
• new sterile tubing and collection container			
• catheter clamp			
• antiseptic solution packet			
• sterile catheter plug			
• sterile drainage tubing cap			
• disposable bed protector			
• disposable gloves			
2. Perform hand hygiene.			

Procedures	Y	N	Comments
3. Provides privacy for resident.			
4. Explains procedure to resident.			
5. Places disposable bed protector under resident.			
6. Opens antiseptic packet.			
7. Puts on disposable gloves.			
8. Ensures new tubing and container are securely connected.			
9. Places them beside old tubing and container.			
10. Clamps catheter shut with catheter clamp.			
11. Using applicator, wipes junction of drainage tubing and catheter with antiseptic solution.			
12. Carefully disconnects tubing. Does not allow any object to touch either catheter or end of drainage tubing.			
13. If resident is going to be disconnected for period of time, such as during bathing, inserts sterile catheter plug into end of catheter.			
14. Covers end of drainage tubing with sterile drainage tube cap.			
15. Does not allow drainage tubing to touch floor.			
16. Disconnects clamp.			
17. If resident is to be connected to new tubing and container immediately, attaches new tubing and container, being sure to maintain sterile condition.			
18. Disconnects clamp.			
19. Removes disposable bed protector and discards.			
20. Removes gloves and discards them.			
21. Covers and positions resident for comfort.			
22. Perform hand hygiene.			
Measuring Output - A Resident Without A Catheter			
1. Explains procedure to resident.			
2. Provides privacy for resident.			
3. Perform hand hygiene.			

Procedures	Y	N	Comments
4. Puts on disposable gloves.			
5. Pours urine into measuring graduate.			
6. Sets graduate on flat surface at eye level.			
7. Reads amounts of urine.			
8. Records amounts of urine.			
9. Observes urine for any signs of blood, dark color, mucus, sediment, or any change from its characteristic odor.			
10. Reports any abnormalities to charge nurse.			
11. Empties urine into toilet.			
12. Flushes toilet.			
13. Rinses:			
• bedpan			
• urinal			
• commode pan			
• special container			
• graduate			
14. Stores them in appropriate area.			
15. Removes and disposes of gloves.			
16. Perform hand hygiene.			
17. Records:			
• amount of specimen measured			
• date of measurement			
• time of specimen measured			
Measuring Output - A Resident with A Catheter			
1. Explains procedure to resident.			
2. Provides privacy for resident.			
3. Perform hand hygiene.			
4. Puts on disposable gloves.			
5. Places graduate below collection container.			
6. Carefully opens drain outlet from collection container.			

Procedures	Y	N	Comments
7. Ensures drain outlet does not touch container or floor. Bacteria could be introduced into container and passed to resident, causing infection.			
8. Allows container to drain completely.			
9. Reattaches drainage outlets to collection container.			
10. Places graduate on level surface at eye level.			
11. Records amounts on intake-output record.			
12. Observes urine for any abnormalities.			
13. Reports abnormalities to charge nurse.			
14. Discards urine in toilet.			
15. Flushes toilet.			
16. Rinses out graduate.			
17. Stores graduate properly.			
18. Removes gloves.			
19. Disposes of gloves.			
20. Perform hand hygiene.			

Checked by: _____

Date signed off *(meets all criteria)*:_____

Chapter 47 Skills Checklists:
Bladder and Bowel Care

Name: _____   Date: _____

Procedures	Y	N	Comments
USING THE BEDPAN			
1. Assembles necessary equipment:			
• bedpan and cover or urinal			
• toilet tissue			
• wash cloth			
• towel			
2. Explains procedure to resident.			
3. Perform hand hygiene.			
4. Puts on disposable gloves.			
5. Provides privacy for resident.			
6. Lowers side rail.			
7. Assists resident in removing his or her lower clothing or raising it.			
8. Asks resident to bend knees.			
9. Asks resident to place feet flat on mattress.			
10. Then asks resident to raise hips.			
11. If resident needs assistance, slips own hands under lower back and lifts.			
12. Places bedpan under resident with seat of bedpan evenly under buttocks.			
13. If resident is unable to assist, turns resident to one side.			
14. Places bedpan against buttock.			
15. Pushes bedpan downward into mattress.			
16. Resident is gently turned back onto bedpan.			
17. Raises head of bed (if allowed) to help resident remain in sitting position.			
18. If resident not able to sit unassisted, stays with resident and holds him or her in upright sitting position.			

Procedures	Y	N	Comments
19. Places top sheet over resident to provide privacy.			
20. If resident can be left unattended, places toilet tissue and call light within easy reach.			
21. Raises side rails, and instructs resident to call when finished.			
22. Disposes of gloves.			
23. Perform hand hygiene.			
24. When resident signals, returns to room quickly.			
25. If resident cannot signal, checks frequently.			
26. Resident should never be left on a bedpan for more than 10 minutes.			
27. Perform hand hygiene.			
28. Puts on disposable gloves.			
29. Assists resident to raise hips.			
30. Removes bedpan.			
31. Covers bedpan. If cover is not available, uses paper towel.			
32. Assists resident, if necessary, to wipe from front to back, making sure that area is clean.			
33. Resident may be turned to side for easier cleaning.			
34. Removes bedpan and takes it to bathroom.			
35. If specimen required or if output must be measured, now is time to do it.			
36. Checks feces and urine:			
• for blood			
• dark color			
• strange odor			
• mucus			
• sediment			
37. If anything abnormal is found, reports it to charge nurse.			
38. Empties bedpan into toilet.			
39. Flushes toilet.			

Procedures	Y	N	Comments
40. Cleans bedpan according to established procedure in facility.			
41. Puts clean bedpan away.			
42. Removes gloves.			
43. Disposes of gloves.			
44. Perform hand hygiene.			
45. Assists resident to wash his or her hands.			
46. Records specimen collected.			
47. Records output if measured.			
48. Records any unusual observations.			
USING THE URINAL			
1. Obtains urinal.			
2. Perform hand hygiene.			
3. Puts on gloves if urinal already in room, since it may be contaminated.			
4. Explains procedure to resident.			
5. Provides for resident's privacy.			
6. Gives urinal to resident.			
7. Assists, if necessary, by placing urinal between resident's legs with resident's penis inside opening.			
8. If resident can be left unattended, places signal cord within easy reach.			
9. Instructs resident to call when finished.			
10. Disposes of gloves.			
11. Perform hand hygiene.			
12. Leaves resident to urinate in private.			
13. When resident calls, responds quickly.			
14. Residents should not be left with urinal for more than 10 minutes.			
15. If resident cannot be left unattended, stays with resident until finished.			
16. Perform hand hygiene.			

Procedures	Y	N	Comments
17. Puts on disposable gloves.			
18. Removes urinal.			
19. Covers urinal.			
20. Takes urinal into resident's bathroom.			
21. Checks urine for any unusual signs.			
22. If specimen or output measurement is required, does it now.			
23. Empties urinal into toilet.			
24. Flushes toilet.			
25. Washes out urinal according to procedures at facility.			
26. Replaces urinal in bedside table.			
27. Removes gloves.			
28. Disposes of gloves.			
29. Perform hand hygiene.			
30. Assists resident with performing hand hygiene.			
31. Records:			
• specimen if collected			
• output if measured			
• any unusual observations			
USING THE BEDSIDE COMMODE			
1. Assembles necessary equipment:			
• commode next to bed			
• bedpan and cover			
• toilet tissue			
2. Explains procedure to resident.			
3. Perform hand hygiene.			
4. Puts on disposable gloves.			
5. Provides privacy for resident.			
6. Inserts bedpan under seat of commode.			
7. Locks wheels of commode if it has lock.			

Procedures	Y	N	Comments
8. Helps resident sit on edge of bed.			
9. Helps him or her put on slippers.			
10. Transfers resident from bed to commode.			
11. If resident can be left unattended, places toilet tissue and signal cord within easy reach.			
12. Instructs resident to call when finished.			
13. Disposes of gloves.			
14. Perform hand hygiene.			
15. If resident cannot be left unattended, stays with resident until finished.			
16. Never at any time use restraints with a resident on a commode.			
17. When resident calls, responds quickly.			
18. Resident should not be left on commode longer than 10 minutes.			
19. Perform hand hygiene.			
20. Puts on disposable gloves.			
21. If necessary, assists resident in wiping, using proper direction.			
22. Ensures that area left clean and dry.			
23. Transfers resident back into bed.			
24. Removes pan from commode.			
25. Covers pan.			
26. Takes pan into bathroom.			
27. Checks feces and urine for:			
• abnormal color			
• odor			
• blood			
• mucus			
28. If specimen or output measurement required, does it now.			
29. Empties pan into toilet.			
30. Flushes toilet.			
31. Cleans pan according to facility's procedure.			

Procedures	Y	N	Comments
32. Returns it to bedside table.			
33. Removes and disposes of gloves.			
34. Perform hand hygiene.			
35. Assists resident with performing hand hygiene.			
36. Records:			
• specimen if taken			
• output if measured			
• any abnormalities			
URINE SPECIMEN			
Routine Urine Specimen			
1. Assembles necessary equipment:			
• bedpan and cover or urinal			
• graduate measure			
• specimen container and lid			
• label			
• disposable gloves			
• paper bag			
2. Explains procedure to resident.			
• explains reason for collecting specimen.			
3. Perform hand hygiene.			
4. Puts on disposable gloves.			
5. Provides for resident's privacy.			
6. If resident is able, has him or her collect sample unassisted.			
7. Instructs resident to urinate in bedpan or urinal.			
8. Asks resident not to put toilet tissue in bedpan, but to put it in paper bag provided.			

Procedures	Y	N	Comments
9. Fills in label with:			
• resident's name			
• room number			
• date			
• time of specimen collection			
10. Takes bedpan or urinal into bathroom.			
11. Pours urine into graduate.			
12. Pours urine from graduate into specimen container, filling it three-fourths full, if possible.			
13. Places lid on container.			
14. Places label on container.			
15. Pours leftover urine into toilet.			
16. Flushes toilet.			
17. Washes bedpan or urinal.			
18. Washes graduate.			
19. Puts them in proper place.			
20. Removes gloves.			
21. Disposes of gloves.			
22. Perform hand hygiene.			
23. Assists resident with performing hand hygiene.			
24. Takes labeled specimen to charge nurse or directly to refrigerator used for lab specimens in facility.			
25. Reports to charge nurse.			
26. Records specimen collection.			
27. Records any abnormalities observed.			

Procedures	Y	N	Comments
Midstream, Clean-Catch Urine Specimen			
1. Assembles necessary equipment:			
• bedpan and cover or urinal			
• graduate measure			
• specimen container and lid			
• label			
• disposable gloves			
• paper bag			
2. Explains procedure to resident.			
3. Explains reasons for collecting specimen.			
4. Perform hand hygiene.			
5. Puts on disposable gloves.			
6. Provides for resident's privacy.			
7. Thoroughly cleans genitals of male or female resident with soap and water or an antiseptic solution.			
8. Asks resident to start voiding.			
9. After stream has started, places collection container under stream.			
10. Catches necessary amounts. It is better not to interrupt stream.			
STOOL			
1. Assembles necessary equipment:			
• bedpan with cover			
• toilet tissue			
• wooden tongue depressor			
• specimen container with lid			
• label			
• plastic bag			
• disposable gloves			
2. Explains procedure to resident.			

Procedures	Y	N	Comments
3. Explains reason for collecting specimen.			
4. Perform hand hygiene.			
5. Puts on disposable gloves.			
6. Provides for resident's privacy.			
7. Has resident use bedpan for bowel movement.			
8. On collection label, writes:			
• resident's name			
• room number			
• date of specimen			
• time of specimen collection			
9. When resident has finished, removes bedpan.			
10. Uses tongue depressor to transfer about two to three tablespoons of stool to specimen container.			
11. Puts lid on container.			
12. Wraps soiled tongue depressor in paper towel.			
13. Discards wrapped tongue depressor in plastic bag.			
14. Empties bedpan in toilet.			
15. Flushes toilet.			
16. Washes bedpan.			
17. Puts bedpan away.			
18. Removes gloves.			
19. Disposes of gloves.			
20. Perform hand hygiene.			
21. Assists resident in performing hand hygiene.			
20. Takes specimens to charge nurse or stores it until it is taken to lab.			
21. Records:			
• taking of specimen			
• any abnormalities observed in color, consistency, odor, or amounts			

Procedures	Y	N	Comments
SPUTUM			
1. Instructs resident to cover mouth and nose when coughing up sputum to prevent spread of germs.			
2. Gets specimen container with lid.			
3. Prepares label with:			
• resident's name			
• room number			
• date of specimen collection			
• time of specimen collection			
4. Explains procedure to resident.			
5. Explains reason for collecting specimen.			
6. Perform hand hygiene.			
7. Puts on disposable gloves.			
8. Provides privacy for resident.			
9. Helps resident sit up.			
10. Instructs resident to breathe deeply several times.			
11. Instructs resident to cough into specimen container.			
12. Avoids contamination by not touching inside of specimen container or inside of lid.			
13. Covers container.			
14. Labels container.			
15. Puts it into plastic bag for transportation.			
16. Disposes of gloves.			
17. Perform hand hygiene.			
18. Delivers containers to charge nurse or refrigerator used for that purpose.			
19. Records:			
• taking of specimen			
• any abnormalities observed, such as blood, thick and sticky sputum, or green color			
20. If resident is unable to cough up sputum, notifies charge nurse.			

Checked by: _____

Date signed off *(meets all criteria)*:_____

MEDCOM TRAINEX®

CERTIFICATE
OF
EXCELLENCE

awarded to

_____

This certificate has been presented to the above named student for successfully completing *"The New Nursing Assistant"* training program.

_____
Instructor

_____
Date

NOTES

NOTES

NOTES

NOTES

NOTES